REACHING RESILIENCE

A Training Manual for Community Wellness

Patricia Omidian, PhD
with
Dionis Griffin
Nina Joy Lawrence
and
Anna Willman

Published by Captive Press Publishing
Eden, NC

This training manual for Community Wellness is produced through the auspices of Focusing Initiatives International, with Melinda Darer, Co-director.

Cover art by Noam Guren. Ilustrations by Nina Joy Lawrence. Typesetting by V.R. Christensen.

ISBN: 978-1976431968

Table of Contents

Biography of Pat Omidian

Dr. Patricia A. Omidian holds a PhD in medical anthropology from the University of California through a joint program with UC San Francisco and UC Berkeley. As a medical anthropologist, she has learned to compare different cultures and their approaches to health. After graduating in 1992, Pat taught for five years at California State University as a full-time lecturer in the department of Anthropology. Her specialty was community mental health and psychosocial wellness.

In 1997, Pat traveled to Pakistan as a senior Fulbright scholar to teach at Pesháwar University in Pesháwar, Pakistan. After her teaching term ended, she stayed to work in community mental health projects for both Afghan refugees and Pakistani communities. In 2001 she was asked by an Afghan non-profit called Coordination of Humanitarian Assistance to help them design a mental health program for their staff that would support their psychological needs. Pat turned to a friend, Nina Joy Lawrence, who suggested Pat use a psychotherapeutic process called *Focusing*. It was the combination of Pat's skills as a trainer and Nina's basic knowledge of *Focusing* that formed the beginnings of her community wellness approach.

In 2002, Pat had the opportunity to design a teacher training/community wellness course for Afghan teachers for the International Rescue Committee, and again she found that *Focusing* was highly effectual. In 2004, Pat, now fluent in Dari, directed the Quaker office of the American Friends Service Committee in Afghanistan (AFSC) for five years. Quakers aim for peace building and reconciliation through group healing. Pat saw individual healing as the necessary forerunner of this aim and found the Afghan office to be a fruitful laboratory of Focusing possibilities with both staff and beneficiaries of the agencies involved. *Focusing* also built a strong sense of community among the staff. Although the AFSC closed its Afghan office in 2008 for financial reasons, many of the people Pat trained still teach and share *Focusing*, in order to continue inner healing for themselves and others.

Before long, Focusing trainers elsewhere noted the success of Pat's approach and asked her advice in taking *Community Wellness Focusing* to El Salvador and Haiti. Two anthropologists saw opportunities of adapting her training to new cultures. Pat's first Focusing colleague, Nina Joy Lawrence, organized an online *Community Wellness* group, which continues to share ideas through a discussion list and online meetings. Mary Hendricks Gendlin, then director of The International Focusing Institute, stated that Pat's approach sparked the core of *Focusing*, which is "a human process that needs to spread." It should not be reserved only for those who can afford the Focusing classes or Focusing-oriented psychotherapists.

Pat has now had the opportunity to teach *Community Wellness Focusing* in thirteen countries including Japan, Mexico, and Liberia. In order to spread this culturally adaptable approach, Pat, with colleague Melinda Darer, founded a non-profit organization in 2014 called Focusing Initiatives International (see epilogue). Several of its board members have helped with this book. Community Wellness projects are currently having success in Central and South Asia, the Caribbean, South America, the Gaza strip, Japan, and various communities of Europe, as well as Canada and the United States. Pat continues to be available for consultation and training, to help adapt these concepts to each unique situation.

-Dionis Griffin

1. RESILIENCE AND PSYCHOSOCIAL HEALTH

I first became interested in psychosocial health as a graduate student in Medical Anthropology in California. I was conducting mental health fieldwork among the Afghan refugee community in that state. The Afghans were very willing to share what they had experienced during the Soviet invasion and occupation of their country in the 1980's. I heard horrific, depressing tales of torture and warfare. After several months of listening, I discovered I was developing my own set of psychosomatic symptoms. I had trouble sleeping and began having nightmares.

Mostly to protect myself, I changed tactics and began asking the refugees what they were doing to cope with their difficult past. Although some Afghans were withdrawn or angry, others managed to be serene and many reached out to help others. What factors made certain refugees resilient in spite of disasters that had made them flee the country? Why were some depressed and others cheerful; some bitter and others friendly? What made the difference?

These questions formed the basis for my future research in Afghanistan. I did find four distinct attitudes that helped these refugees be resilient:

- Belief in a higher power (in this case, belief in Allah).
- Recognition that their experience was shared by others and was not a personal attack.
- Hope for the future and hope that their children would have a better life, even if the parents were suffering.
- A willingness to help others and to acknowledge that there were others who had an even harder time.

The question then became, are other communities resilient in the same way? What examples of resilience exist in a culture, in spite of difficulties? Is it possible to teach people to be more resilient? This workbook is a result of 24 years working with these questions.

What is Resilience?

Resilience is that wonderful ability to bounce back after severe setbacks. It enables survivors of war and natural disasters such as earthquake, drought and flood to survive not only physically, but to find personal peace. To survive physically, a person must have food, water and shelter. But even with those needs met, some are crushed by the burden of emotional stress and the breakdown of the community. The surprising thing is that there are others who, in the same circumstances, are not so severely affected.

Another word for resilience is "psychosocial health," meaning the successful blend of both psychological and social adaptations. Although there are numerous organizations which serve those in crisis and are skilled at providing emergency needs, these same organizations are less prepared to provide "psychosocial health." For one thing, this need feels less pressing than food and water. It may not be visible until the initial crisis has passed. Also, although many may be suffering, this need seems to be an amorphous, many-headed problem almost impossible to treat.

One reason this need seems difficult to treat is that the suffering populations are numerous and most often, poor. When there are large groups of people in desperate circumstances, as in Liberia during the outbreak of Ebola, the usual methods of health care are overloaded. The medical community is stretched to the maximum. There are numerous injured and sick, but there are also a number, even greater, of panicked citizens who are afraid and anxious and who urgently need information on how to protect themselves and their families. Such a community in crisis needs a low-cost, locally administered program that can be easily replicated in every other community. Such a program needs to be easily learned and able to be taught by non-professionals.

As a medical anthropologist, I bring the special understanding that such a program also needs to be culturally appropriate. If it does not fit cultural norms, it will not be accepted by the local population. Communities are resistant to outside interventions, often because they are perceived as "Western." Some communities actually become hostile and drive aide workers out. Others are not able to benefit from Western technologies, because their infrastructure is absent. Many cultures have taboos against sharing problems with strangers, and will not participate. Finally, many non-profit organizations do good work at first, but the positive results last only as long as the founders remain directly involved. Once those dynamic individuals move on, the program fades.

Reaching Resilience solves these problems, first and foremost, by having built-in ways for each activity to be adapted to the community's culture. When a facilitator can tap into the unique resilience of a culture, the community begins to "own" the program and local leaders want to teach it. Furthermore, *Community Wellness Focusing* (our term for this approach) can be easily taught. It has a track record of being continued after the initial teacher has left and even after funding has stopped. The cost of starting this program is low—only the cost of the workbook, a flipchart, markers, some optional handouts, and a good initial teacher.

Focusing

One challenge in teaching psychosocial wellness is the question of how can one deal with emotional problems effectively and at low cost? As has been previously discussed, most people cannot afford professional fees. Many others are hesitant to share difficult emotions; there may be cultural barriers that prevent them from doing so. In Afghan culture, particularly, sharing personal information is taboo; it's simply not done. The best thing I have found for dealing effectively and privately with emotions is *Focusing*, a process uncovered during 30 years of research and practice in psychotherapy and which has received five awards from the American Psychological Association.

Focusing is a practical way of bringing psychological help to a broad variety of people. This natural process, discovered by psychologist and philosopher Dr. Eugene Gendlin, is now practiced by thousands throughout the world through training by The International Focusing Institute and other Certified Focusers. *Focusing* allows deep work on psychological issues without breaching ethical dilemmas of trust and disclosure. Focusers have complete control over what is shared and they draw upon their inner understanding for their healing process. (See www.Focusing.org. Also Chapter 4, "Focusing: A Calm Place.") There is no need to talk to a professional or relate details of one's life story. Participants are invited to sense their own inner body-wisdom, with the recommendation to hold any feelings that arise in a calm, safe place, and to welcome all feelings, even unpleasant ones, as honored guests. By sensing an open place inside, people can create an internal area that allows them to find new possibilities for solutions. There is the suggestion of finding new small steps that "sit right" for the individual.

Another aspect of *Focusing* is training the companion, who learns to listen to another in a way that creates a therapeutic atmosphere. The companion practices listening without judgment or comment, only by offering a compassionate "presence." Facilitators especially need to model this type of listening in their workshop discussions, by welcoming all the participants' contributions and making sure that every person feels accepted and heard. It helps if the facilitator has some prior experience with *Focusing*. Fortunately Focusers and Focusing Trainers, certified by The International Focusing Institute, are now located in many parts of the world, and these make good facilitators for teaching Resilience.

Regardless of their training, a facilitator needs to use three main skills. A good facilitator will 1) pause frequently in the conversation to give the participant time to think and reflect. The pause often elicits more information, even if it initially seems uncomfortable. It is a silent but welcoming presence that invites communication. If a pause doesn't produce more information, the facilitator can 2) repeat back something of what the participant just said. This reflection indicates that the facilitator has been listening and is truly interested in learning more. Often when people hear their own words spoken back, they open up with a deepening of that information. Finally, a good facilitator needs to 3) have a warm, welcoming presence. Hopefully this is part of his or her personality, but facilitators can also benefit by reading about "Presence" in Chapter 7. Part of being present is to be aware both of one's own inner sensing and the inner sensing of the speaker, at the same time, and in a gentle uncritical way. It is to have an open mind and an accepting spirit.

In spite of this detailed discussion of three Focusing skills, prior knowledge of *Focusing* is not mandatory. When I started teaching *Focusing*, I had learned how to focus from a friend, but had had no formal training at all. I was given long-distance guidance from The International Focusing Institute and from a few skilled Focusers. Even more importantly, participants who have taken the workshop that this book is based on have often felt adequately trained to go on and train others in the same methods. So prior Focusing experience is not essential. Sometimes facilitators have, at some point, taken on-line courses with the Institute, which require no travel and are therefore not too expensive. However, I emphasize that *Focusing,* in spite of its brand name and courses, is a naturally occurring process in all human beings. It is a skill we knew as children, so for most people, it is simply recognizing and improving something they already possess.

How to use this workbook

Reaching Resilience is meant to be used in the field while actually teaching. Its purpose is not only to help distressed communities but also to train you, the facilitator, to understand and introduce the various concepts. The beginning of each chapter discusses the main concept behind the activities. A story illustrates that principle so that you can visualize it in action. At the end of each discussion are suggested activities for the students, which you are invited to adapt, through open discussion, to the needs of the community, always coming back to the principle or concept being introduced.

While these activities have been successful in many cultures, you will need to 'tweak' or fine-tune them to fit your particular group. The key to doing this is to let the class members discuss a principle and come up with their own adaptations. You will need to keep an open mind about solutions and allow each group to find its own way. The participants will teach each other what is relevant and what isn't. They will let you know what helps them towards psychological health.

This flexibility is important, not only because cultures vary, but also because the type of participant varies. Sometimes the class members will be traumatized citizens who are unaware of customs other than their own. At other times, they will consist of aide workers, teachers and other educated professionals. Sometimes the class will be large and sometimes it will have only three or four participants. The time allowed will fluctuate also. Some workshops will last several days; some only an evening.

The activities in this workbook are arranged in a certain order, but this order will change depending on the participant's needs and the amount of time allotted. I myself have never done the activities in the same order twice. In addition, many activities have multiple sections and you can select which ones you wish to use. My vision is that every culture will eventually create its own workbook that reflects its unique values, as has been done in Afghanistan, Pakistan and Gaza. *Community Wellness Focusing* should mirror each distinct community's reach for Resilience.

* * *

For more information:

Focusing Initiatives International
www.focusinginternational.org

The International Focusing Institute
www.focusing.org
*To find *Focusing* trainers worldwide, click on "Learn Focusing," then on, "Find a Certified Focusing Professional"

Activity 1: Interviewing for Resilience (for the Facilitator)

If you have time before your workshop begins, interview some local people. Interviewing will give you practice in listening skills, and you will also learn how local people are coping with disaster, which will influence how you teach your workshop. Look for those people who have shown resilience. Talk to local non-profit organizations; they will know who is doing well in spite of everything. Two questions you might ask such an organization are: Who is unusually happy and at peace? Why is this so?

Seek out those who are doing well and talk to them. The people you interview may provide examples of local solutions to problems. You can use the information you gather in your workshop.

Example of a possible Interview:

Questioner (Q): I heard from (name of agency) that you are doing well, in spite of the disaster.

Community Member (CM): I don't know. They say that. I just carry on.

>   **Q:** (Pause. Repeating key phrase) You just carry on?
>
>   **CM:** I have my prayer rug and I pray many times.
>
>   **Q:** (long pause. Interviewer nods but says nothing.)
>
>   **CM:** I pray for my family, for my friends.
>
>   **Q:** (repeating key idea) So...you pray for everyone.
>
>   **CM:** No, not everyone. Just people with problems. We all have problems. I've seen many problems.

Q: (long pause. Questioner nods sympathetically.)

CM: You have to think of the good things.

Q: (repeating) The good things?

CM: When I pray, I always thank God for the good things. Like a roof over my head and the fact we didn't argue yesterday—no fights! It was wonderful.

Q: (Repeating) No arguments! That *is* wonderful. (Genuinely curious) What do you do when there *are* fights? (Etc.)

2. INTRODUCING AND FACILITATING THE WORKSHOP

From the beginning of your workshop, you want to create a welcoming atmosphere. Of course you will need to attend to details, such as explaining what the course is about and describing the manner in which you will be working. But you want to interweave those details with an accepting mood, a *Focusing* attitude of openness, and a willingness to hear from everyone, not the least of which is to sense your own feelings as sincerely as possible.

In a way, your job is to let your students teach each other. Let them know that when it comes to their personal challenges, they are the experts, and that they already know a great many solutions for their community's problems. You may want to establish some rules for the workshop; the best way to do this is to have the participants make them. As they share their hopes and fears (see Activity 2B in this chapter), you will all need to figure out a way to keep the class emotionally safe.

How do you help people find their own solutions? As an anthropologist I have learned there is great power in going into a community with no goals and no agenda, only with a pencil and a notebook. I listen to what people say and write it down. You don't have to be an anthropologist to do this. You will find a treasure trove when you are open to what others share.

There is also an established method for promoting group participation called Dynamic Facilitation (DF). It outlines a way to lead a group that is meeting around some problem. Briefly, you first ask them to share what they already know. While I cannot cover all of DF here, the following story about how I used its principles might be helpful. At the end of this section, further reading is suggested.

In 2014 I went to Mexico to meet with a Montessori school that was having problems. The teachers were in conflict and it was beginning to affect the children. I spoke no Spanish and was not familiar with their problems but I decided to use Dynamic Facilitation to help them address their problems.

Over the course of three weeks, I met with the teachers three times. I should add that a fellow Focuser, Cintya, and I twice met individually with the one teacher who seemed to be feeling the most negatively about the situation, and in our second session (a Focusing session) this teacher started to feel positively towards *Focusing* and towards the future of the school. We then met as a group, and during this hour I introduced myself and my fellow Focuser from Mexico, and we asked what they wanted to work on. Cintya made a list of their concerns on a flip chart. I asked the teachers to bring something in writing to the second meeting that included their vision for the school.

The second meeting lasted for three hours and used *Focusing* and Dynamic Facilitation. The teachers started by reading what they had written and sharing their vision of the school with each other. We were surprised, because their concepts were absolutely in sync and they agreed with each other completely. Using *Focusing*, we asked each person to sense what they felt inside about the problem situation. They all took a moment, closed their eyes, and checked inside to see what was blocking their shared vision, and again we wrote everything on a flip chart.

From this list, a goal was selected for them to concentrate on. It was easy to see that most of the blocks were around problems in communication between the teachers, so that became the topic. One person said, "Maybe I'm starting too soon," and she gave us her list of all the things that were making her crazy. I wouldn't let her name names.

I had been coaching Cintya on Dynamic Facilitation and it got to the point where she could lead the group in Spanish without having to stop and translate for me. I could sit back and let her carry on, because I could tell what was happening from body language. I instructed her not to let the participants talk directly to someone in the group, but to talk only to her. That was key; it meant the talk didn't become personal, but was always directed toward the facilitator.

Cintya was good at saying, "Did I capture this right? Is there more here? Is this what you meant?" Every person was given their say until they felt understood. That is another key point—the facilitator has to make sure everyone gets heard. At the end of talking, each person had to state what he or she saw as the solution to the problem. We wrote the solutions on another page. That was a third key point. A solution had to be given, no matter what the excuses.

At the end, there was a real shift. The teachers all liked the solutions; they were in sync, and some of the solutions were already happening because they were talking to each other. My lack of Spanish, knowledge of Montessori schools, or details of the situation were unimportant, because Cintya and I had facilitated a dynamic discussion in which everyone participated. The process may sound simple, even easy, but it does take some skill to facilitate.

The main point is that we created a situation where these teachers taught each other and discussed problems with each other. We made sure everyone had the space to express how they felt. We gave them time to feel understood. Then they developed a common goal and proposed their own solutions. Our main contribution was to model and to encourage the *Focusing* attitude, which is to listen carefully, with acceptance, while keeping in touch with inner feelings.

As you work your way through the Introduction to your Workshop (Activity 2A), you will need to explain the *Focusing* attitude, what it is, and how they can use it with each other.

Then you can choose between these two activities described below:

1) "Hopes and Fears"—which involves setting up some class rules, or

2) "What Problems does your Community Face?"—which assesses the expertise of a professional group.

Your choice will depend on whether you are facilitating a community in crisis, or professionals who will be facilitating a community in crisis. Both activities allow you to put some basic elements of DF into practice.

* * *

For more information:

From Conflict to Creative Collaboration: A User's Guide to Dynamic Facilitation by Rosa Zubizarreta. Two Harbors Press, Minneapolis, MN, 2014

Activity 2A: Introduction to the Workshop

<u>Materials</u>: Name tags (optional), flipchart, and markers. Handout 2A—for groups of professionals (located at the end of this chapter); and a handout showing the course objectives if you have made one. You might want your participants to bring journals so they can write down their reactions and impressions of the class.

<u>Time</u>: 30 minutes

* * *

A. Welcome:

Welcome the participants and introduce yourselves as the trainer or facilitator. Talk a bit about your own journey with *Focusing* and *Community Wellness.* Tell them that *Focusing* is not a "Western" construct, but rather a natural human capacity that can be enhanced by a good facilitator. *Focusing* will teach them to listen to themselves and to each other in ways that support emotional growth and social cohesion. It will help them deal with their emotions in a safe, yet healing way. Explain that you will describe *Focusing* in more detail later in the course. But for now, they need to understand that the Focusing attitude is one of listening and acceptance.

Note to trainer: Remember it is always best if your sharing comes from within you, from your inner sensing. In this way you model *Focusing* and your inner body wisdom.

You also need to include technical details, such as:

    a) when you plan to start and finish,

    b) how many days the workshop lasts,

    c) what to do during meals and other breaks, and

    d) the level of commitment you need from the group.

B. Introductions

Let facilitators and participants introduce themselves and say a sentence or two about themselves. Give each person a chance to speak. You might want them to wear nametags. Learning each other's names can relax the group. Let introductions be fun. Psychosocial wellness needs to include all the emotions and it certainly should include laughter.

Some ideas for making it fun:

- In a small group, go around the room with individuals introducing themselves. Ask them to say one thing about themselves that people might not know. Examples: I like to write stories. I like to eat Japanese food.

- If possible have them rhyme their name. Example: I'm Mary, red as a cherry.

- Do a clapping game. Example: "Clap clap I'm Pat." The group echoes, "Clap clap she's Pat." "Clap clap and I'm Barbara." The group echoes again, "Clap, clap she's Barbara." Then on to the next.

- Have people introduce themselves in pairs and share something about themselves with a partner. Then each person can introduce his or her partner by name to the large group.

- In very large groups (50+) it often works to have people introduce themselves to someone in the room whom they have yet to meet. And then that pair finds another pair (whom they don't know) and introduce

- themselves. Next, this set of four goes to any other group in the room and they introduce each other. In this way, there are at least eight people who now know each other.

C. Objectives of the Course

Introduce the general outline for the course including the course's objectives. You could prepare a handout. These objectives will change from workshop to workshop, but may include the following:

- Participants will develop skills for promoting community resilience and wellness that are appropriate to their culture.
- They will develop *Focusing* skills in listening both to themselves and to others.
- They will learn positive coping skills that will reduce violence and decrease stress and trauma as experienced in different segments of society.

For a professional group, you might have this list:

Sample list of outcomes for the end of the workshop

- Know and be able to share some *Focusing* skills.
- Understand what is healthy and normal for their community.
- Understand the value and range of emotions.
- Understand the role of Resiliency in Mental Health.
- Be able to share what they have learned in their communities.

D. Way of Working

Explain your role as a facilitator. You are not the expert on their psychosocial health. You have some skills which you will share, but you expect that they also have a lot of expertise that they will also share. Your job is to model and teach the *Focusing* attitude in order to encourage them to talk and to help them feel understood.

In the same spirit, you expect them to meet their needs in this course–for instance, to leave if they need to use the bathroom, or if they need a break from the emotions inside them, to relax for a moment, or even to take a nap.

Activity 2B: Hopes and Fears

<u>Goals:</u> To allow the participants to share their concerns about this course and alleviate any fears. Also to get feedback that will help you tailor this workshop to their needs, and to create together a list of rules that will help everyone feel safe. This activity is geared towards the average participant.

<u>Materials:</u> Flipchart and markers, tape

<u>Time:</u> 30 minutes: 10 minutes in pairs, plus 20 minutes for feedback

* * *

To begin, tape two blank flipchart pages on the wall. Label one HOPES and the other FEARS. Alternatively, you might label them WANTING and NOT WANTING.

Divide the group into pairs and ask each pair to talk about what they are hoping for and what fears, if any, they may have about this course. Since this workshop is about emotions, encourage participants to include real fears. Give examples like:

- I am worried that I will have to say my feelings out loud.
- I don't want to have to think about unpleasant things.
- I don't want others to know what my problems are.

Of course you want to give examples also of real hopes:

- I hope I will learn something that will help me sleep better at night.
- I hope to be able to do my job better.

After ten minutes, ask each pair to share one "hope" from their discussion. Write it on your flipchart. After every pair has participated and each "hope" been written, ask if there are other hopes not on the list that they would like to share with the group.

Then ask each pair to share one "fear" and put each one on the other flip chart. Ask if anyone would like to add a "fear" not yet listed. As they mention fears and concerns, there can be some discussion in the group about the process and some reassurance to allay these fears.

Go through some of the hopes and explain how *Focusing* can help.

Go through the fears and talk about how people can keep themselves safe.

Develop a list of rules. This list may include:

- You are responsible for deciding how much you share.
- What is shared here must stay confidential. We don't ask what specific issue comes up for people in their *Focusing*.
- You are in control when you are *Focusing*–you decide what you want to say. Only share what feels comfortable.
- We appreciate each person's contribution. *Focusing* is about acceptance. We want to develop an accepting attitude towards ourselves and others.

Remind the class that confidentiality is a critical component to psychological and psychosocial programs. Confidentiality means that you never talk about what a person says to you. You can talk about the process or the activity, but never talk about, nor inquire into, the details of someone's life.

You might end up with a printed list like this to put on the wall:

Rules for the Workshop
Because we are talking about and looking at our own emotions,
we need to feel safe.

- You can share *techniques* learned here.
- Anything *personal* said in this room stays in this room.
- If you don't want people to know something, don't tell them.
- Get what you need out of this course.

Note to trainer:

You will want to model the companion role in *Focusing* by taking time to really listen to people when they share hopes and fears. You can also model *Focusing* by reflecting back the images and feelings in what they say, pausing for more to come as people check inside.

Example:

> **Workshop participant:** I want to get something I can use from this workshop. I'm worried it might be like other workshops where nothing stays with me to use in my work or my life.

> **Trainer:** Ah, you are worried this might not be useful, and you really want to have something you can use in your work or your life. (Pause...)

> **Participant:** Yes, something I can practice enough that I can do it next week maybe.

I think of Dynamic Facilitation as *Focusing* in a group. When *Focusing* by yourself, you want all your parts to be given equal respect and heard equally.

When doing Dynamic Facilitation, you want all the participants to be given equal respect and to be heard equally. As they see you welcoming this attitude in the group, it will make it easier for them to welcome it in themselves.

Activity 2C: What Problems Does your Community Face?

Goals: To help participants see they are the experts concerning their community's problems; also to help you learn their range of expertise and custom-design the course in consequence. This activity is geared more toward the professional participant, like aide workers, teachers, NGOs, etc.

Materials: Flipchart and markers; handout for each participant

Time: 30 minutes

* * *

Discussion: Invite participants to describe the kinds of problems and issues that their communities face. Write these on the flipchart.

Lead the discussion and accept all ideas in brainstorming fashion (see Chapter 11, pg. 144 for a description of brainstorming) to get the group warmed up and used to talking. The idea is to accept everything that is said and write it down without any comment or criticism. People are willing to talk about shared problems, like war. Avoid personal questions about individuals in the group, but if someone shares a personal story, that's OK, and take time to listen.

Note to trainer: This process helps the group know that they have a great deal of knowledge to share. In this alternative activity, you will note that, although you ask them to list problems, you are not asking for solutions. That is because you will be finding solutions together throughout the rest of the workshop. At the end of your time together, you can re-post your list and ask the group what solutions seem available now.

Handout 2A: About You

1.	List key community problems.	
2.	Describe your community work.	
3.	What do you hope to learn from this program?	
4.	How do you want to share what you learn when you return home?	
5.	Please give us your job title and years of experience.	
6.	Have you facilitated a workshop? If yes, what was the topic?	

3. CULTURAL NEEDS AND DIFFERENCES

I went to teach in Pakistan in 1997 at a University in Peshawar. Although somewhat familiar with the culture, I was totally unprepared for the traumatic effect of war. Men, women and children—refugees from the 30-year Afghan war with the Soviets—were continuously entering from the mountainous border. Afghans told me of family members who had died in blood feuds over land or politics, of fathers and grandfathers who were killed or who disappeared in political disputes or from random attacks or bombings. Few could remember life without war and they all had traumatic stories to tell, of death, loss of home, or livelihood.

I could see homemade tents of blankets or tarps draped over a rope, everywhere in Peshawar. Parents were struggling to find ways to meet their families' basic needs and keep their children safe and well. Luckily schools were available in the camps and urban areas. For instance, the International Rescue Committee (IRC) maintained a number of girls' schools, but the teachers were not trained to respond to the psychosocial needs of the children. Besides, they had psychosocial issues of their own, because they were refugees as well.

Because of my background working with Afghan refugees in California, I felt I could improve the teachers' own psychosocial health. A colleague and I searched the traditions and literature in Afghan culture for evidence of the resilience we sensed lay underneath the trauma. We wanted the training to blend with the local values and tap into the healing power of the community itself. We knew that relying on the community's own expertise—rather than on my professional insights or externally imposed solutions—would empower the participants the most and open the door for Community Wellness.

Participants brought their own skills to the course and developed trauma recovery modules that were specific to their communities and which they could implement themselves. Later, in Aghanistan, a team of dedicated leaders trained eight student interns each year to enter schools and teach *Community Wellness Focusing* and other psychosocial subjects. Each intern trained approximately 200 teachers per year, thus reaching 1,600 teachers. In addition, these same leaders taught community-based workshops, so that from 2004 to 2009, over 3,000 civilians in six provinces were trained. I still receive reports that many of these projects continue even though funding for them has ceased.

Below is a diagram used by the World Health Organization (WHO) to demonstrate five levels of mental health services. It shows the importance of a community workshop like ours in Peshawar. Such a psychosocial workshop can reach the lower levels where most people reside; it is also affordable and easily taught by non-professionals. (For reproducing purposes, this triangle can also be found at the end of this chapter as Handout 3B.)

As the WHO triangle in the diagram narrows, the cost of mental health services goes up (the vertical arrow on the right) and the number of people served goes down (the vertical arrow on the left). Most people, the ones at the base of the pyramid, must rely on their community or themselves for low-cost or no-cost care.

The pyramid for physical health services is similar to the one for mental health. The majority of people, pictured at the pyramid's base, take care of themselves or receive informal help. One example is the case of the common cold. Many people around the world cannot afford to go to a store. They also may not have transportation. They are helped, if at all, by friends and family, who may suggest a remedy based on common household items.

A smaller group of cold-sufferers—but still a significant number—are able to purchase an over-the-counter remedy. For mental health or stress reduction, one might learn yoga, join a prayer group, or take a free self-help class. But for many, there is limited access even to these services.

On the next layer, a subset can obtain services at a local clinic, and this Primary Health Care provides medication and/or people trained in mental health. If one has a cold that does not get better with over-the-counter help, one goes to the clinic or doctor for treatment. For mental health, one could go to a mental health clinic. Yet most of the world has no access to such clinics.

The smallest group, at the top of the pyramid, receive highly skilled medical care from specialists and psychiatrists, who are usually located only in large population centers and who charge high fees. Back to the example of a cold. If the cold persists and turns into pneumonia, one goes to a hospital for care. In mental health, only a tiny portion of people receive this kind of service. Statistically speaking, top professionals serve a very small percentage of the population. Yet according to WHO projections, one in three individuals will need mental health help in their lifetime. Therefore, what is done at the individual and community level is critically important.

Keep in mind that mental health is a broad term that covers a variety of ailments. Psychosocial health, which many professionals believe can prevent serious mental health issues, can be more narrowly defined. Isn't it the ability to fit in socially, find friends, and mingle with the local population? In other words, isn't it an acceptable adaptation to the norms, whatever they may be? Obviously then, psychosocial wellness looks different in different cultures. Normal behavior in one country may be unacceptable in another. Participants in our workshops find it useful to understand that concept.

Facilitators too need to understand this. A successful psychosocial workshop is one which appeals to and resonates with the local culture. When the subject matter feels as if it embodies a society's unique values, those who learn the principles feel empowered to use them and to teach them to others. Thus, the workshop reaches more and more people and creates a growing amount of Community Wellness.

The following activity will help your group understand their society's cultural positioning and to gain some perspective on what "normal" and "wellness" really mean. I have noticed that once participants start talking about what is "normal and acceptable," they also start talking about what is "non-normal" and "unacceptable." They find it helpful to know that sometimes cultural deviations are signs that someone, especially a child, is in psychosocial trouble. For instance, if a ten-year-old in the US is unwilling to play with his peers and prefers to stay with his parents, he might be having psychosocial difficulties, but the same child among Afghan refugees would be considered normal. In the US, adults would help such a child become independent, but in Afghan refugee camps, the same child would be praised.

Geert Hofstede conducted respected research in this area, and his theory of Cultural Dimensions divides a culture into many segments. Cultures have been compared and evaluated in each of these areas. The Hofstede Center states that a culture often determines values, and values often determine behavior. Therefore, to properly understand behavior, it is vital that we understand cultural differences.

Four useful dimensions are:

1. Collectivism vs. individualism: Do people prefer to live in ones and twos, or collectively in groups? Afghan society prefers collectivism and so it is normal for the extended family to live together. Everyone in an Afghan society values the group; if a young adult is eager to live alone, he is considered abnormal. In the USA, the reverse is true. A young adult is expected to leave his family and the elderly also prefer to live on their own.

2. Large power distance vs. small power distance: Are people distant from each other on the basis of status and power? In Afghan society, power usually brings certain privileges to heads of government, directors, parents and elders. People with high power would not defer to those with less power. By contrast, in the United States the power distance is small. The government gives equal rights to individuals and values each. People with high power can easily meet and interact with small power people and leaders' ideas are often challenged or rejected by people of less power and influence,

3. Risk avoidance vs. risk taking: Do people in society take risks and perform activities with uncertain results or do they prefer to stay safe? In Afghan society, people tend to take risks which can cause great danger. Many Afghan refugees have traveled across perilous mountains. In the USA, on the other hand, safety seems to be a prime concern, and there are many rules designed to ensure it.

4. Emotional expression vs. emotional control: Does a society value free expression of emotions or the control of them? In Afghan culture, people value controlling their emotions. They often hide their feelings, especially negative ones. For example, they may try not to show their tears. On the other hand, it is acceptable for a man to show anger. In some societies, people are expected to be volatile and the expression of emotions is encouraged, so people show their feelings and discuss their problems more openly. They show anger and tears, and hug each other freely.

The main point is that there is no specific "normal." There's nothing "wrong" with hiding or not hiding one's tears: there's nothing wrong with living in a group or living alone. Every subsequent discussion in your workshop should include some reference to your group's cultural norms. Your participants may find it easiest to see with children, who, under stress, often act outside the norms, or outside their own norms. Usually somebody in the room will say, "Oh, that's my son!" Or "This child in my classroom has suddenly become good. We need to talk to this child."

What can be hard in the following activity is that participants often know only their own culture; they have nothing to compare it to. I let them introduce stereotypes of foreign cultures but I don't let them use ethnic differences. I may say, "Let's pick something less loaded. Something from a Bollywood movie." Mainly I want them to consider what is normal for themselves. I try to keep the discussion from being an "us versus them" type of action. Don't try to change their prejudices, just change the conversation.

* * *

For more information:

To learn more about the Hofstede Center's findings on cultural differences, visit: http://geert-hofstede.com/cultural-dimensions.html

Activity 3: Psychosocial Wellness

<u>Goals:</u> Participants learn to define Psychosocial Wellness and normalcy. They also learn to identify the four key markers that show how wellness is defined in their community.

<u>Materials:</u> Flipcharts and markers of four different colors (if possible), tape, and copies of handouts 3A and 3B found at the end of this chapter (optional).

<u>Time:</u> 40 minutes

* * *

Discussion and Definitions:

Lead the whole group in a discussion of the following:

- What do we mean by "normal"?
- What do we mean by "wellness"?
- Do these terms vary by area, culture, or language?

Brief Explanation:

Psychosocial Wellness is:

- When one is able to make the most of what one has, in a positive way.
- When one can deal positively with problems and traumas in life.
- When one is flexible so that when problems come, one is able to master them in a creative way.

Ask for examples from the group to illustrate each point. Then tell them you are going to show them one way to determine cultural differences. Draw four horizontal lines on the flipchart to indicate the spectrums or ranges of four different cultural dimensions, and label them as indicated in the following four boxes. As you draw and label, explain what each line means.

Line 1: Group vs. Individual Focus

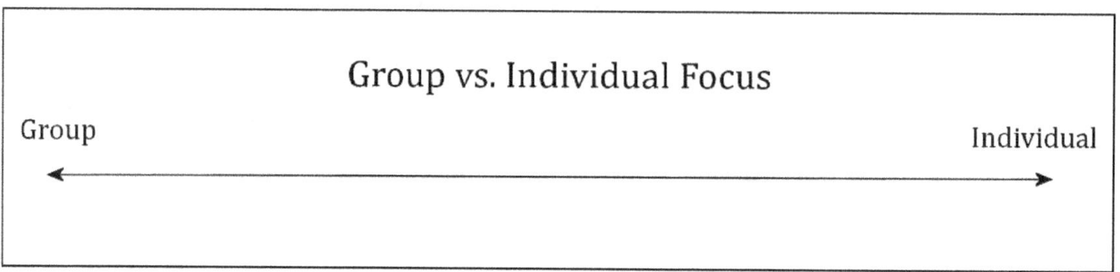

Explain the following:

- Group focus means:
    - You assume from birth that people belong to groups so problems are shared. Consequences are shared also.
    - You value harmony within your group so you would not share a problem outside your group.
- Individual focus means:
    - You assume that people look after their own interests.
    - Less value on harmony; you assume disagreements and conflict will occur.
    - Problems are seen as personal and not affecting others.

Line 2: High vs. Low Power Hierarchy

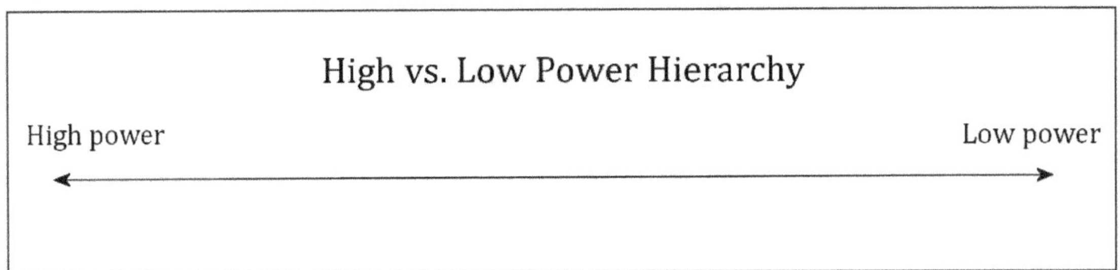

Explain the following:

- High hierarchy or big power distance means:
    - Differences in power are expected, accepted.
    - Power brings privileges.
    - Power holders are inaccessible.
    - Authority cannot be contradicted.
- Low hierarchy or small power distance means:
    - Differences in power not well accepted.
    - Value on equal rights.
    - Power holders accessible.
    - Disagreements expected.

Line 3: Taking vs. Avoiding Risks

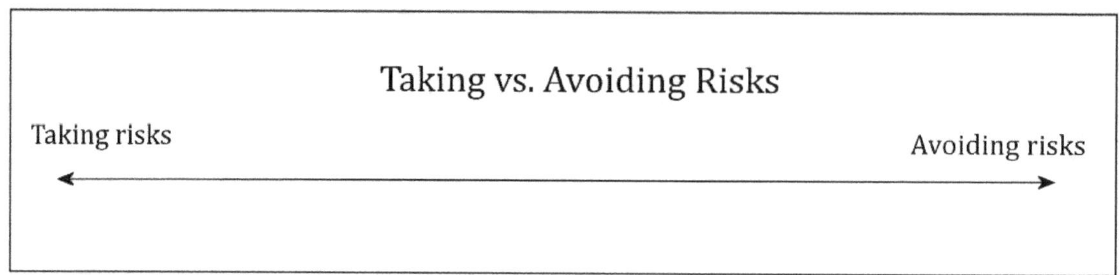

Explain the following:

- Risk Taking means:
  - Unstructured situations and personal risk are accepted as normal.
  - You prefer open ended objectives.
- Risk Avoidance means:
  - You prefer situations that are clear, predictable.
  - Precise answers and objectives are preferred.

Line 4: Emotional Control vs. Emotional Expressiveness

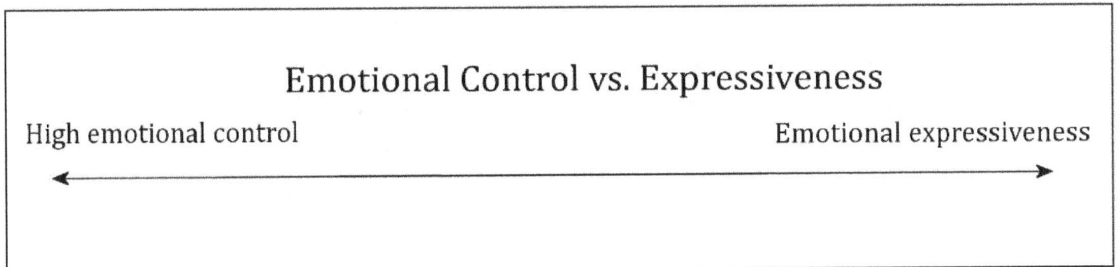

Explain the following:

- High emotional control means:
    - You are expected to contain your emotions, especially negative ones.
    - Value is placed on self control. During disagreements, emotions are put aside.
    - Tears are not acceptable.
- Low emotional control means:
    - It is normal to show a range of emotions, including negative ones.
    - Conflict is resolved through open discussions with lots of emotion expected.
    - Tears are allowed.

Discussion:

Ask the group to reflect on their own society. Why is it important to understand what is normal? Refer back to psychosocial wellness and how people need to adapt to the positive aspects of their own society in order to be socially healthy.

Ask: "If a person ______ (add an emotion, like "gets angry", "sheds tears"), is it normal?" Fill in the blank and see if it sounds normal. Change the gender and see if it sounds normal. Ask them why.

Next, look at each line by gender and age. Ask the group to identify where on these lines they would place MEN, WOMEN, BOYS, and GIRLS in their culture, giving a different colored mark on the spectrum for each category. In other words, each mark should represent where the group feels that their community falls. Is it more on one side or the other?

Note to trainer: You will find an optional handout (#3A) at the end but don't distribute it until after the discussion, so people can find their own way. It is important to encourage the members of your class to come up with their own experiences. Ask them to think of sayings, turns of phrase and local stories that support this activity. You want them to find out what is 'normal' in their culture.

These concepts can be difficult to grasp, especially by people who know only their own way of doing things. Give time for the group to think it through. If the group is large, divide them into smaller groups of three to five people for discussion. After 15 or 20 minutes, have them come back together, and let a spokesperson for each group share what they discovered. Be willing to take time and review the concepts as many times as the group needs.

You may contribute examples from other cultures for contrast. You may cite examples from the movies. You may share your experience with the target culture, but be careful not to make judgments as you do so. I always use something from my own culture that they know as a stereotype, like the fact that Afghans think U.S. parents don't care about their kids since they kick them out when they are 18. Remember there isn't one correct answer. A culture is fluid, and so is the outcome of this activity.

Handout 3A: Defining Normal

1. What is normal: Collectivism or Individualism?

Collectivism:

- Assume from birth that people belong to groups so problems are shared.
- Value harmony; people may not disclose problem if it's about family.

Individualism:

- Assume that people look after their own interests as a person moves toward independence.
- Problems are seen as personal and not effecting others.
- Less value on group harmony.

2. What is normal: High Power Distance or Low Power Distance?

High Power Distance:

- Differences in power are expected, accepted.
- Power brings privileges.
- Power-holders inaccessible.
- Cannot contradict authority.

Low Power Distance:

- Differences in power not accepted.
- Value equal rights.
- Power-holders accessible.
- Disagreements expected.

3. What is normal: Avoiding risks or taking risks?

Avoiding Risks:

- Prefer situations that are clear, predictable.
- Structure and precise answers and objectives preferred.

Taking Risks:

- Unstructured situations and personal risk are accepted as normal.
- Like open-ended objectives.

4. What is normal: high or low emotional control?

High emotional control:

- Contain one's emotions, especially negative ones.
- Value placed on self-control and disagreements must put emotions aside.
- The expression of certain emotions, such as crying, is discouraged.

Low emotional control:

- Emotionally expressive.
- Normal to show range of emotions, including negative ones.
- Open discussions good for resolving conflict.
- Tears are encouraged.

Handout 3B: Triangle of Optimal Health Services

4. FOCUSING: A CALM PLACE

We have already discussed some Focusing skills: pausing during conversations, reflecting back what is said, and making sure everyone feels understood. These are the Focusing qualities of social interactions. But being aware of our internal signals is the core of *Focusing*. The power of *Focusing* reveals itself when we begin to sense the wisdom in our bodies. This inner wisdom is key to making peace with our difficult emotions and creating a way forward that allows us to grow and learn. It is key to feeling better. To sense the wisdom inside us requires a slower pace than we usually give ourselves in our hectic lives. Taking time to pause, having someone reflect back what we have said, being aware of our bodies, all help us slow down and sense inside.

Focusing is a natural process that everyone is born with. We can notice children doing it. If you ask a child if he wants a drink of apple juice or orange juice, he might look up at a corner of the room and say, "Ahhh." He is sensing the apple juice in his body. Then he might look down at the floor and say, "Ummm," as he senses the orange juice in his body. Meanwhile, if you are like most parents, you say, "Hurry up, make up your mind." You are, without realizing it, asking him to abandon the slow sensing of his physical sensations and make a decision based on thinking. Inadvertently, you are teaching him *not* to focus on his inner wisdom, but to rely on reason alone.

The inner process named '*Focusing*' was re-discovered by the world of psychology when Dr. Eugene Gendlin, philosopher and psychologist at the University of Chicago, decided to take a closer look at psychotherapy. In the

1960's he started to research the question, 'Why do some people get better in a course of therapy and other people do not?' He audiotaped many therapeutic sessions. Rather quickly, he and his graduate students learned that they could tell from the very first session who was going to benefit and who was not. To their surprise, it wasn't anything the trained psychologist was doing. It was what the clients were doing *inside themselves.*

The successful client talks in a certain way. He pauses more often. He hesitates. He seems to consult some inner sense—something which he finds hard to put into words. By contrast, the unsuccessful client talks easily and quickly. She communicates what she already knows and confines herself to the facts in her head, whereas the first client searches for words and images that haven't been in his awareness before. Rather than finding intellectual solutions to her problems, the successful client senses how the whole situation feels in her body and finds words from this.

Dr. Gendlin wondered if there was a way to teach this skill to those who did not already use it. Through trial and error he came up with a six-step method of learning *Focusing* that is still in use today. His seminal book, "*Focusing,*" describes this method. Others have built on this extraordinary work, taking his steps and adapting, changing or expanding what he started. For example, Ann Weiser Cornell developed a form of *Focusing* she calls "Inner Relationship *(IR)* Focusing." In this method, any emotion or physical reaction noticed in a person can be described as a "part" or a "something in me" and the Focuser develops a relationship with that "part." This allows the Focuser to approach many kinds of problems or issues with an attitude of curiosity, and with less likelihood of feeling overwhelmed.

In our modern era, we "know" that thinking occurs in the brain and the brain is in the head. But centuries ago, this fact was not obvious. Instead, it was believed that thinking occurred in the heart or the stomach, maybe both. *Focusing* recognizes that our inner wisdom is often sensed in the chest and stomach area. It turns out that, while reason does take place in the brain and is particularly useful for logical, orderly problems, our inner wisdom, located in the core of our body, is useful for finding solutions to emotional and other kinds of problems.

When I arrived to teach in Peshawar, Pakistan, I knew nothing about *Focusing*. I only knew I wanted to serve at a local non-profit organization called Coordination of Humanitarian Assistance (CHA) in Afghanistan/Pakistan. The director asked me to develop a program to help his staff, many of whom were under a great deal of stress that was affecting them both physically and emotionally. Debriefing, or the process of helping aid workers cope with the emotional stress of their work, was standard procedure in the Western world, but such service for workers was rare with Afghans. Yet the staff had faced grave dangers. Many of the men had been imprisoned, beaten or tortured and they found it difficult to keep the resulting anger and other emotions out of their family life. Female staff had also been harassed and beaten by the Taliban or their rivals, the United Front forces. In interviews, most spoke about the difficulty in doing their work because of flashbacks, intrusive thoughts, non-directed anger and depression, and fear of the future.

From long experience in the region and with those who had resettled in California, I knew that standard therapy or Western debriefing methods would not work. Afghans cannot air secrets about their families or their workload to others. It is just not allowed. I needed something that did not require the sharing of personal information yet could still heal inner wounds. When I talked about this problem with my American colleague, Nina Joy Lawrence, she told me about *Focusing*, which allows deep work on psychological issues without the focuser having to reveal any details. The Focuser has total control over what is shared. Those being treated can focus on their psychological problems either alone, or with a listener who only reflects back what is said and who need never know the nature of the problem. *Focusing* can also be done in a large group with one person leading. It was a model that would fit the culture and also not need a lot of introduction.

To help *Focusing* fit the culture even more, Nina Joy and I found local literature and sayings that supported inner sensing. Every culture probably has something similar if you look for it. The American culture talks about "trusting your gut feelings." The French writer Pascal said, "The heart has its reasons that reason doesn't know." Einstein said, "The intuitive mind is a sacred gift and the rational mind is a faithful servant. We have created a society that honors the servant and has forgotten the gift."

My initial attempt at teaching *Focusing* to non-profit staff was a success. The staff reported that levels of tension and anger at work decreased. CHA's director said that the managers' problem-solving abilities improved. One manager stated, "Old family issues and old pain about the war were weighing me down, always increasing my tension and anger. Now that is much better. The pressure is less." CHA staff felt that *Focusing* helped them cope. They also felt new hope for the future in spite of the worry and uncertainty of their lives.

Soon after, I was employed by CHA to teach some refugees, and still later, by the International Rescue Committee, to teach *Community Wellness Focusing*, We found that *Focusing* helped the mental health and wellness of the whole community, as many participants shared what they learned with friends and family.

Because many with whom we worked carried so much pain and trauma, we found they did not feel safe at first going inside. They spent much of their energy staying away from feelings, emotions, memories, and body reactions. As I started one session, I asked people in the room (all Afghan refugees living in Pakistan) if they knew of a calm place where they could do this inner work. Several said that they had no calm place in their lives and no beauty. So almost by accident, I started this session of beginners by asking them to *imagine* a calm, beautiful place in their lives. If they did not know such a place, maybe they could think of someplace they would love to visit—calm, beautiful and safe. I discovered that this activity, called *A Calm Place,* is a wonderful way to start Focusing training, especially when the participants have never done *Focusing* and don't know what it is. (Although sometimes I start with the attitude of gratitude in Chapter 10.) I have also used *A Calm Place* to end a workshop, which allows everyone to come away with a positive feeling.

A competent facilitator will enhance the group members' natural *Focusing* capacity, but I stress again that you must introduce Focusing in a way that matches your target community's culture.

In addition, because this activity is such a crucial part of the program, I recommend you practice leading *A Calm Place* with just a few individuals first, outside the group, so that you feel comfortable facilitating it. I also recommend that you let your group experience what it is like to go inside in a calm, safe way, *before* attempting to describe what *Focusing* is. *Focusing* is best understood by experiencing it; most people find it very difficult to define.

* * *

For more information:
Focusing by Eugene T. Gendlin Ph.D. (Bantam Books, NY, 1981)
      www.focusing.org

The Power of Focusing by Ann Weiser Cornell, Ph.D (New Harbinger Publications, CA, 1996)
      www.focusingresources.com

Activity 4: A Calm Place

Goals: By the end of this activity, participants will be able to describe what it is like to do a *Focusing* activity. They will be closer to experiencing a calm, safe, and/or beautiful place inside themselves. This inner place will be each person's retreat, from where other activities can begin.

Materials: Flipchart, markers, copies of Handouts 4A and 4B (optional) or two blank pieces of paper per student, or have them bring their journals.

Time: 40 minutes

* * *

A. Finding your Calm Place Inside

In times of crisis, many people feel they have no safe place in their lives into which they can retreat to rest and recharge themselves. Sometimes there are few calm places of beauty. But one place is always available and that is a calm place inside yourself. You can call it whatever you like (or call it whatever you need) but the point is to see how it feels to be inside yourself in a calm, quiet way.

48

Tell them some people cannot go into such a place the first few times they try, but eventually everyone does. If they can't do it the first time, that is OK. Tell them to take time and be kind to themselves; that is what matters.

Guidance:

The activity is simple. Slowly read the statements below (which are also in the Handouts). The activity works well when led by the facilitator and every one follows what is said.

> *I'm bringing my awareness into my body:*
>
> - *Starting with my feet...*
> - *Then my legs...*
> - *Back...*
> - *Arms, shoulders...*
> - *Head and...*
> - *Into my center (my throat, chest, stomach area).*
>
> *I'm sensing this calm place in me...*
>
> - *I'm sitting in this place...*
> - *I'm sensing how this place feels...*
> - *I'm sensing where I feel this safe place in my body...*
> - *I'm inviting it to stay with me as I come back...*

Note to trainer:

- Before everyone starts, invite them to imagine a place that is calm and beautiful.

- Once people are inside, give a minute's pause between each suggestion.

- Take several breaths between each suggestion. This will give time for people to try what you suggest.

- Feel yourself doing what you suggest.

- It is important to watch the group as they do this for the first time. You will be able to tell who is able to stay with it and who needs help.

- It's OK to offer possibilities to those who are having difficulty, such as suggesting a mountain glen or a place by a lake.

- Let everything a person feels be a plus, even pain. Someone may say something like, "I found some pain and could not get past it." Suggest that they greet each pain or feeling that comes, offering a simple 'hello,' before moving forward.

- If they still can't get past it, suggest they take a moment to allow the pain just to be. Or suggest that they view it as if from the outside. They stay aware of it, but leave it and move on.

- Be encouraging, but don't make promises. Everyone's experience will be different.

Discussion:

After the activity, take a few moments to allow the participants to bring their attention back into the room and the group. Then ask some questions:

- Did anyone fall asleep? If so, congratulate them. They were relaxed!

- Who did *not* go to the place they had chosen? For those who feel you did *not* find a calm place, describe what did happen. Did it help you relax? Most people get to their safe place as they develop trust in this process and as their body is ready. There is no such thing as failure in *Focusing*, because it is a process or a journey.

- How did it go for the rest of you? Can you describe what you saw? What did it feel like in your body? Encourage descriptions or images. Where did you feel it? Encourage participants to share only what feels right for them.

Two more questions could be:

- What was difficult?
- What did you like about the exercise?

Note to trainer:

I don't start by calling this place "safe" (some people cannot find a safe place), but I do ask if they find peace there.

When someone says afterwards they were not able to do it (and a number of people will say this) let them know that is normal. Check to see how far they were able to go. Many will have noticed some subtle changes. Others may be able to relax even if they cannot imagine a calm place. It's still good to relax! One person kept saying he couldn't find such a place, so I asked if anything had changed. He said, 'Nope, but it was a little less noisy." Such a change is encouraging.

For people who have been through trauma, this activity is a healthy place to start dealing with the inner healing process. It will locate a place where some inner peace and space can come in the midst of overwhelming emotions. For some people, it is calmness; for others it is safety or beauty.

Remember this is only a beginning. They are trying something new. It's like riding a bike—not everyone learns on the first try. Help them to be open to anything that comes. We want to notice and nurture, also to be aware of and encourage any body feelings that we find in the inner place.

B. Drawing:

Distribute Handout 4A with the "body" drawn on it. Or distribute blank paper. Then direct them to draw a picture of their calm place.

After the group has drawn their pictures, explain that this inner place is theirs. Whatever they want to call it, they can go there anytime they need it. It is at this time that I tell the group that they have just had a *Focusing* experience. How their bodies feel as they are imagining being in the calm place is called a "felt sense" and is the core of *Focusing*.

Invite participants to list under their drawing some of the ways they think *A Calm Place* activity would be useful in their day-to-day lives. One advantage of this drawing activity is that it can show you who has and who hasn't understood the concepts.

C. Find ways this activity can fit into your own culture:

Have a flipchart and markers handy as you explore how people can re-define and adapt this activity to their own culture and values. You might ask the following:

- In what ways does your society/culture/local tradition find peace and calmness inside? (Write responses for the group to see.)
- Would anyone like to share a local story/poem/saying/proverb that matches what we have just done? (Again, record what is shared.)
- Invite participants to bring in local stories/poems/sayings/proverbs that illustrate any activity done in this workshop.
- Make a catalogue of what is shared.

As an example, there is a saying in Islam: "Allah is closer to you than the vein in your neck." It means you are not alone and Allah knows your innermost places. In Christian cultures, the Holy Spirit is described as "always with us." Usually there is some way this calm, peaceful attitude is encouraged by every culture.

D. Explanation: What is *Focusing*?

This is your chance to tell more about *Focusing*. Explain that it is a process of being with what's inside us. Let the group know they may have times when they experience a range of feelings—sadness, disappointment, fear, anxiety, or satisfaction. *Focusing* allows them to be in touch with these feelings without getting caught up in them. It also puts them in touch with a source of healing that comes from within. *Focusing* can help:

- Be with difficult feelings.
- Be more accepting of yourself and others.
- Learn to listen to each other and create a better work or home atmosphere.
- People who say they get very angry, very sad, or very scared, have said they receive emotional balance by *Focusing*.
- People have said that it helps them talk to God or Allah from their hearts better than before.

Focusing is a simple way to pay attention to inner sensations and feelings. It creates a place of wisdom inside us and also a place for hurt. It is not a new idea; it is not a Western construct. There are many practices in every society that point to *Focusing* and we can discover them in this workshop.

The *Focusing* process includes various steps, the simplest being the Pause. We pause for the length of several breaths to sense what is happening inside and how we feel. With a pause, our attention can be brought to our innermost place so we can sense our body's understanding. We can also take a problem or event and look at the "whole thing" and check our inner response to "the whole situation." This gives us access to greater wisdom than our thoughts alone.

The ability to pay attention to the inside places brings us greater resilience. The activities you will be participating in over the next few days will help you learn to cope with your emotions and feelings, and help you listen to others, family or friends, colleagues or students, as they work through their own feelings. You will learn to be with yourself—and others—with no judgment, no bias, and no goals. You will learn to create a gentle space inside yourself for holding it all.

Note to trainer:

This is a brief description of *Focusing* and it is important not to spend too much time on it. It is best to learn *Focusing* by doing it. You can, and should, refer to these points again at later times in the workshop

E. Homework:

Distribute Handout 4B and invite the group to practice this activity in the evening at home. Encourage them to explore all the imagined places where they feel safe, and the feelings each place creates inside their body.

If this form cannot be duplicated, have your participants copy the it into their journals or onto a piece of paper, so they can also take the activity home to practice.

You might ask participants to teach *A Calm Place* to one person in their home or work or neighborhood.

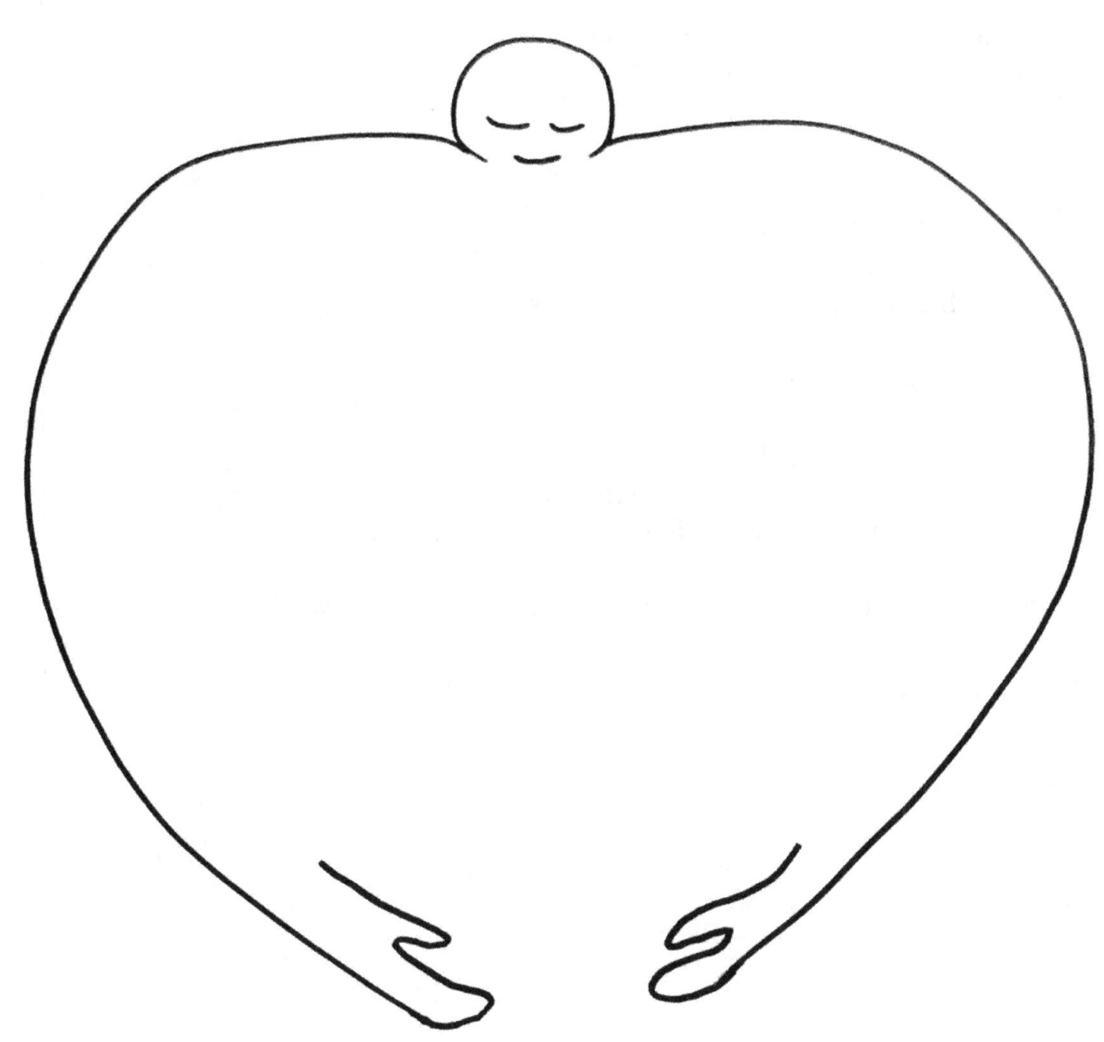

I'm bringing my awareness into my body,

- Starting with my feet,
- Then my legs,
- Back,
- Arms shoulders,
- Head and
- Into my center (my throat, chest, stomach area)

I'm sensing this *calm* place in me...

- I'm sitting in this place...
- I'm sensing how this place feels ...
- I'm sensing where I feel this *beautiful* place in my body...

I'm inviting this feeling to stay with me as I come back.

5. STORIES OF RESILIENCE: POSITIVE DEVIANCE

In December of 2013, the Ebola virus was identified in West Africa and by spring of 2014 it had spread to Liberia. The following July, I became part of a World Health Organization team (WHO) combatting the epidemic. The deadly outbreak was spreading fear and panic among citizens in the region and beyond. WHO was concerned because fleeing villagers, already infected with the virus, could carry the disease into larger cities and across international borders.

My job was to gather information on local practices that either spread or hindered the disease. I was also tasked with assessing psychosocial issues in the affected communities. This included helping medical personnel, many of whom had good reason to be fearful.

At the WHO office in Liberia I started a *Focusing* class for some colleagues. Once again, I was amazed at how quickly *Focusing* enables people to become more resilient, and how easily it allows fear to dissipate.

Let me share with you exactly what I did in a 45 minute session. The first thing was to say, "Tell me how your body is right at this moment." One at a time, they described their body feeling—such as tired or stomach bubbling or achy or energized or hungry—and then I asked them to notice if there was more, and each person added to what they had said. We talked about how there is often more underneath what we might first say.

Next, I led them within themselves very slowly, taking lots of time to sense into each area of the body as we moved toward the center, i.e., into the chest and

stomach area. Once inside I invited them to sense something they were grateful
for and then to feel how *that* felt inside. All noticed that the world fell away and
they became comfortable in their bodies. One man in the group said he was
aware of his aches and pains until he felt grateful—then they just faded away.

Next, we went inside again but this time we *started* with feeling grateful. Once
everyone was grounded in a grateful feeling, I invited them to bring in "all about
Ebola and Liberia and themselves in this situation." After sitting with this for a
bit, I invited them to return to their place of grateful appreciation. After this
exercise, when people spoke about what happened, they all noted how much
smaller and less overpowering the Ebola situation felt when it was surrounded
by appreciation for other things. One said that a thankful feeling was a lifeline
out of the heaviness of all the problems. Another said that it was like Ebola was
small and was really encircled by something more powerful. Yet another said
she realized she was thankful that Ebola was not as bad as predicted. (See
Chapter 10 for more about gratitude.) Everyone felt better at the end of the 45
minutes. Even more, they felt connected and grounded to each other. I could
feel the shift in the room and I felt grateful for the gift of *Focusing*, which could so
quickly calm our fears and bolster our resilience.

One of the things I looked for as I searched for local practices that spread or
hindered the disease, was some story of local resilience. If I could find even one
story among the Liberian people of one person who, on their own, had
successfully dealt with the disease, it would be like discovering a gold mine.

There were some challenges to this search. For one thing the local populace was
stressed and afraid. They didn't want to talk about Ebola. Many had taken to
saying, "Ebola is not real," and I was sure it was because it was scary beyond

belief. Cars with loudspeakers drove around the city saying, "Ebola is real." But so many rumors were flying around that it was hard for the average person to see what was what. Official information was scarce and it was even difficult for me to answer people's questions.

Another challenge was that, for our safety, the World Health Organization had many rules to follow. When visiting people in the communities, we were not allowed to go into their houses or shake their hands. We were to stay at least one meter away at all times from those with whom we spoke. I felt as if I could not be warm and myself under such constraints. I could not touch these people, and this is a country of people who like to touch and be in physical contact. A local person told me, "Ebola is a disease that can only be stopped by *not* being kind, by putting aside compassion. We are told not to touch our sick loved ones. How can we do that? How can we not comfort someone we love?" But to touch someone who is ill with Ebola can be a death sentence for the caregiver.

Through persistence, we finally found a local person who had figured out how to be safe and still care for others. She used only locally available materials— things like plastic bags and bleach. This meant that people didn't need to wait for medics to arrive in safety suits. They didn't need to be given expensive materials they couldn't afford. They could take positive action on their own and care for each other. This is of great importance for community resilience and morale.

Taking her example and some others, we were able to make videos, posters, and training materials, as well as TV and radio broadcasts to spread this key information. We trained people to train others, such as church groups. My colleagues developed a four-pronged training: proper hand-washing, how to make chlorine water for washing and purifying, how to wear long sleeves and put rubber gloves or plastic bags over the hands while caring for the sick, and how to take off and dispose of the used items safely.

As a medical anthropologist, I know how important it is to discover what is already working in a given situation. A few resilient people who are coping surprisingly well can hold the key to helping the rest of the population. In development work, such an example is called *positive deviance*, a term developed by Jerry and Monique Sternin to refer to unusual but local solutions to complex and seemingly unsolvable problems. To discover examples of positive deviance, you must observe the culture and query the local population. You need to identify those in the community who are faring unexpectedly well. You learn from those individuals, adopt and adapt their strategies, and help share their experiences with others.

The following two activities can help identify those who might have "positive deviance" characteristics which can lead to community wellness. Choose between the two, depending on how much time you have, or according to your preference.

* * *

For more information:

The Power of Positive Deviance: How Unlikely Innovators Solve the World's Toughest Problems by Richard Pascale, Jerry Sternin and Monique Sternin,. (Harvard Business School of Publishing, MA, 2010.)

Activity 5A: Stories of Resilience

Goal: By the end of this module participants will have learned resiliency stories from their community, their family and themselves.

Materials: Copies of Handout 5A or blank paper, writing utensils

Time: 20 minutes

* * *

Recognizing Resilience:

In small groups of two or three people, have the participants complete Handout 5A with stories about instances when they, their family, or their community have reacted positively to stress. Next have them share their stories with each other. Working in small groups will give each person time to talk. As they tell their stories to each other, they will become aware of how resilience has allowed hardships in their own communities to be addressed in positive ways.

Discussion:

After the groups come back together, ask a few people to share one of their stories, either about themselves, their family, or their community. Highlight the key points on a flip chart, noting that resilience exists, and they can find it if they look for it. Sometimes the facilitator will need to help participants identify resilience by reframing or summarizing what has been said. Be sure to emphasize the last two points from the following sample list, because sometimes trauma causes people to avoid emotions, and this avoidance of emotions can cause psychosocial problems. Remember to point out that being able to experience all the emotions is part of resilience.

Note to trainer: This activity needs little supervision. Participants may ask whether they must only give examples from when they themselves were present. Tell them that any story is good, even if it happened before they were born or while they were away.

Sample List of Key Points

- Having a goal to live for
- Resourcefulness
- Curiosity and intellectual mastery

- Selflessness toward others
- Compassion with detachment
- The desire and ability to help others

- A vision of the possibility of restored and orderly civilization
- Remembering and invoking images of good things
- Remembering cultural sayings, such as: The green stick does not break when it is bent

- Having a full range of emotions, both positive and negative
- Being in touch with a variety of emotions

Activity 5B: Positive Deviance

Note: The second activity is similar to the first, but takes more time and is more thorough because it compares those who do well with those who don't do well. It also explains the term "Positive Deviant".

Goals: By the end of this module participants will have an awareness of resilience within their families and communities and will be able to identify ways that they know people are doing well in spite of trauma or hardships.

Materials: Flipchart, markers, 1 or 2 copies of Handout 5B for each person (a participant may want to fill out more than one handout), writing utensils, and tape for fastening lists to the wall.

Time: 45-60 minutes

* * *

Start this activity by explaining that this is actually a search for those "*Positive Deviants*" in their community or those who do well in the face of trauma and hardships. In every community there are people who are socially and psychologically healthy, even though they share the same hardships as everyone else. We call these people the 'positive' members of society. They are often fewer, compared to the many who have not yet recovered emotionally or socially. Because they are fewer, we can say that they deviate from the norm. All have experienced similar trauma but the *Positive Deviant* has managed to thrive, recover and be healthy. Each one provides a model for finding a way forward in a stuck situation.

Give Handout 5B to each person. Let them know they can fill out more than one if they wish. Invite each person to think of at least two people they know who have gone through terrible times. It is not necessary to use one's own experiences in this activity. I often recommend participants think of stories of other people, rather than look at their own lives. This gives them some emotional distance from traumatic events. Of these two people whom they know, one should be a person who has never recovered emotionally and/or socially. The other should be someone who is now emotionally well and has a positive spirit. Give them time to reflect.

On the handout (or blank paper) write:

- What happened to each person?
- Four qualities that show you why you think each person did or did not do well.

Divide into small groups of two or three. Have them share both the stories and the signs of wellness (or lack of wellness) that each person has identified. Have them discuss:

- What happened to each person on their handout.
- What qualities show which one is doing well or not doing well.
- The difference between these two people.

Hand each group a marker and a blank piece of paper. I like to give them each a large page from the flip chart. Have them make a list of the positive traits which they have discovered.

When all groups are ready, have a spokesperson from each group present their findings before the large group. The lists can be taped to the wall of the room, so that everyone can see them.

Discussion:

After presentations, lead the large group in a discussion of common ways in which people identify wellness and resilience.

- What are the common traits of wellness?
- How many people in your community do you think are "well"?
- How were they helped to be well?
- What do you think supports wellness in your community?

I often walk around and circle the common points on each list. I might make a new list on my flipchart of points that one group found important and others missed. I may add new points as they find traits previously overlooked.

Note to trainer: The purpose of the activity is to let people see that some within their community maintain psychosocial wellness in the face of the hardships and trauma. The second purpose is to find out *how we can know* someone is doing well. Contrasting those who are doing well with those who are not doing well helps in this process. Be sure to refer back to the culture's norms for psychosocial wellness (Chapter 3).

Some may say: I am the *Positive Deviant*! If they do, encourage them to say more—how do they know they are well both socially and psychologically? It's helpful if others have also noticed these traits. It may be that you know differently, that this person is struggling to be well. But be encouraging and positive and accept the person as they describe themselves.

Handout 5A: Stories of Resilience

Self	In Family Relations	In Community Relations

Handout 5B: Positive Deviance

Someone who is not doing well	
The story of Trauma	Four qualities that show that someone is not doing well.
Someone who is doing well	
The story of Trauma	Four qualities that show why someone is doing well.

6. INNER GUESTS

Many cultures around the world value guests and consider being a host an honor, even if it is onerous or inconvenient. In addition, many spiritual traditions value spending time going inside and getting to know one's self. The Muslim culture has a tradition of valuing both, and it turns out these values together give a wonderful entry into *Focusing*.

> *This being human is a Guest House.*
>
> *Every morning a new arrival,*
>
> *A joy, a depression, a meanness,*
>
> *Some momentary awareness comes*
>
> *As an unexpected visitor.*
>
> *Welcome and entertain them all....*
>
> *Be grateful for whoever comes,*
>
> *Because each has been sent*
>
> *As a guide from beyond.*
>
> By Rumi
>
> Translated by
>
> Coleman Barks

As an anthropologist, I always look for ways that new concepts will be accepted by the local culture, and the concept of "welcoming inner guests" came about almost accidentally. Muslim prayer culture has a tradition of sensing inside in a calm, non-judgmental way. So my colleague Nina Joy Lawrence and I looked for local sayings and writings that would reflect this inner sensing. Nina Joy found several poems by the classic Persian poet Rumi, in which he described something like *Focusing* eight centuries ago. The poem that seemed most apt described a Guest House, but not just any guesthouse. This Guest House is a metaphor for getting to know one's self.

Rumi's poetry is well accepted in Afghanistan, where he was born. We found that many Afghans, even illiterate villagers in remote areas of the country, know his poems by heart. That culture does not encourage people to display or explore their emotions. But writing or reciting poetry allows even the toughest man to express his tender side. It was not uncommon for a local participant in our workshops there to recite a poem or even to create one on spot.

As for guesthouses, many Afghan families keep a special room, separate from the family rooms, especially for guests. This room has the nicest furniture and carpets, the newest pillows and mats. Early American culture had a similar room called the "parlor." So the Afghans are comfortable with the idea of treating inner guests with honor, as if "sent as a guide from beyond."

Over the years I have continued to use the concept of an inner Guest House, and not just in Muslim cultures. The metaphor works well in many cultures. Any belief system that values hospitality can appreciate a poem about guests, and the poem's gentle approach helps us understand that we can welcome our inner visitors. Rumi's poem even provided a wonderful entry into the Japanese culture when I taught *Community Wellness Focusing* in Japan.

The important thing for this first workshop was that the use of Rumi's poem helped my participants realize that *Focusing* is not a Western or American concept. It is a universal concept, part of their past. It helped them "own" *Focusing*; the Pakistani even renamed it, "Standing at the Door of God." A participant in our first workshop said, "*Focusing* is in the history here. It is in the literature, the poems. Our prophet even sat in the cave before becoming the messenger of God doing something like *Focusing*. So what have we been doing these 1000 and more years? Why doesn't everybody know this?"

Because *Focusing* seemed part of their culture, the Afghans who learned it felt comfortable teaching it. They spread the concept willingly and naturally. Several agencies in Afghanistan continue to teach it, using the Dari language manual that was developed in 2002. Some local non-profits now work with the Ministry of Education to train pre-school and primary school teachers in this process. Manuals have been developed in the Urdu and Pashto languages also.

Focusing reached not only the cities but also the countryside, as demonstrated in the following story. To help you understand the situation in the story, I want to point out that after 30 years of war and centuries of tribal conflict, violence in Afghanistan is a common way to solve problems. It can earn a man status and power, even though it is also recognized as a sign of unhealed trauma. It would have been a mistake for my workshops to try to change this aspect of their culture. People would have stopped coming, or might have blocked us from returning. People don't like to feel their norms are under attack. Then they refuse to listen, even to something they actually want to learn. Nevertheless, as the following story shows, sometimes violence is resolved through our teachings. This story was told to Nina Joy Lawrence by Muqueem, who taught *Community Wellness Focusing* in Mansur's village.

> One villager, we will call him Mansur, often fought with his
> neighbors about whose turn it was to use the irrigation water.
> One day his neighbor took water on Mansur's day. Mansur
> yelled and tried to change the water flow. His neighbor hit him

with a shovel. Mansur ran home to get his shamsher (big knife) and shaloq (big stick).

Suddenly Mansur said, "What am I doing? Maybe this anger I feel is a guest! Maybe I should focus now, and after that I will go out to fight."

Mansur decided to focus. He sat on his toshaq (cotton mat). He got quiet, holding his head in his hands.

Mansur spent some time with his inner "guest." He sensed the fighting spirit inside him and it showed him what it felt like doing. It felt like hurting or killing his neighbor.

He could feel something else in him, something that DID NOT WANT TO DO THAT!

His body calmed. Mansur left his weapons and went out. He met his neighbor in the field. Mansur said, "I'm sorry. I will get water the next day. You are like my brother. If I didn't have food, you would feed me."

His neighbor said, "What happened? You were like crazy! Now you are normal, like a brother."

Mansur replied, "It was a guest, not really me. I've learned how to listen to my guests. I learned *Focusing* from Muqeem."

His neighbor asked to learn *Focusing*.

The village decided to build a *Focusing* house together, in thanks for ending the terrible squabbles. Listening to inner guests in a *Focusing* way can bring peace.

* * *

For more information:

This module is based in *Inner Relationship Focusing*, which was developed and described by two focusers in collaboration:
      Ann Weiser Cornell http://focusingresources.com/
      Barbara McGavin http://www.focusing.org.uk/barbara_mcgavin.html

For more on the traditions of violence and its social impacts, refer to *The Performance of Emotion among Paxtun Women* by Benedicte Grima (2005)

Note on Rumi: *Wikipedia says Rumi (1207 –1273), was a 13th-century Persian poet, Islamic scholar, theologian, and Sufi mystic whose "influence transcends national borders and ethnic divisions. [Numerous nationalities] have greatly appreciated his spiritual legacy for the past seven centuries. His poems have been widely translated into many of the world's languages."*

Activity 6: Inner Guests

Note: This activity should only be done after participants have experienced the Calm Place in Chapter 4.

<u>Goals:</u> The purpose of this module is for the participants to begin to focus with whatever comes. They learn that the relationship to their inner selves works best when they are calm, caring and non-judgmental.

<u>Materials:</u> Paper and colored markers and/or crayons, copies of Handouts 6A, 6B and 6C.

<u>Time:</u> 45 minutes

* * *

Guest House Focusing

In the large group, read Rumi's Guest House poem aloud, either the short or the long version (in Handout 6A.) Then lead a discussion about the poem from a psychosocial view. Note that it is possible to use this poem as an example of how to encourage us to be with emotions, felt senses, body pains, and anything inside.

We can think of our reactions to events and our body-sense of certain situations in our lives as "visitors." Guests and visitors are not permanent residents—they come for a short time and leave. Some stay longer than others. Some annoy us and some bring us joy. But in many traditions, how we treat each guest is important. A welcoming approach allows us to form a relationship with whatever feeling comes. Explain that we often start just by finding a comfortable place to be near it.

A. Practice Inviting Guests

Have participants stand in a circle, so that they have room to move a bit if they wish. Say something like:

- Close your eyes.
- Imagine you are home and there is a knock on your door.
- You go to the door and open it.
- A guest is there; someone you really want to see.
- Sense how you feel about this person.
- Notice how your body reacts as you see and welcome this guest.
- Sense where in your body you feel this.
- Take a moment to take it in.
- Find a word or phrase or gesture that fits what is inside you.
- Now open your eyes.

Invite participants to share their experiences, using their bodies to illustrate where appropriate and comfortable.

After a few minutes of discussion, ask the group to close their eyes again. This time:

- There is a knock at the door.
- It is a guest that you really do *not* want to see.
- Sense how you feel about this person.
- Notice how your body reacts as you greet and welcome this guest.
- Sense where in your body you feel this.
- Take a moment to really take it in.
- Find a word or phrase or gesture that fits what is inside you.
- Now open your eyes.

Again, invite participants to share their experiences. Ask them what is different this time?

Allow the group time to process both events.

B. Coming into the Guest House

Invite the participants to sit down however they are comfortable. Lead the participants into their Guesthouses by inviting them to close their eyes (or look down at a place on the floor). Say something like:

- First notice your breathing—paying attention to it coming in and out
- Now bring your awareness down to your feet, and sense how they are
- Bring your awareness slowly up your legs, pausing at each place to sense how each part feels. You may want to sense how the chair (or floor) supports your body and take time to lean into that support
- Now move your awareness slowly up your body, to your back… hands… arms… shoulders… and head…
- (*pause*)
- Bring your awareness into the center of your body, going first to your calm, safe place, sitting there and noticing how your body feels in that place…
- Now, invite any inner guests, whatever wants your attention now…
- When you sense something, whatever comes, say 'hello' to it. It might be a body feeling, an image, even an emotion…
- Whatever it is, just take some time to find the best way to describe how it is in your body…
- (*pause*)
- Now see if it's OK to just be with this guest with interest and kindness…
- Maybe sense if it has a feeling or emotion…
- Let it know you are willing to hear it…

- (*pause*)
- Now I invite you to find a word, phrase or image that describes it... Maybe you can even let the guest know that you are willing to let it come back...
- And check in your body to see how it feels now compared to what it felt like before...
- Take a moment to thank your body, and your guest...
- (*pause*)
- Slowly bring your attention back out, notice again your hands and arms... your legs and feet... the chair (or floor) where you are sitting. And when you are ready, you can open your eyes...

Discussion:

Invite participants to share anything that feels comfortable from their experience of these activities. Maybe ask them:

- How did a guest come in?
- What was it like to bring it into your Guesthouse?
- What feels different now?

C. Drawing:

Offer paper and colored pencils or pens and give participants the chance to draw a picture of their Guesthouse. They may also want to draw whatever guest is present in their Calm Place or what it feels like inside to spend time with the inner guest. After they draw, let each participant share something about their picture. In this way, you can tell whether they are understanding how to use *Focusing* or whether they need more help.

Note to trainer: You can break down the goals for this *Focusing* activity into 5 parts. You want the participants to:

1. Experience their own Guesthouse and identify inner guests.
2. Notice body felt-senses and welcome them.
3. Locate words or metaphors that give them a handle for dealing with their stress or trauma.
4. Develop a relationship with an inner guest.
5. Practice *Focusing* language i.e. use words that show acceptance of all that comes.

Keep the activity positive. Reassure those who were not able to meet guests that it takes practice and some people take longer than others. Often many years of avoiding what one feels means it is harder to notice what does come.

As you invite people to share, be careful that you don't probe into the story behind the guest. Let people know that they are welcome to keep their lives private. *Focusing* works just as well without sharing the details. One advantage of the Guesthouse is that people can use metaphors or images to describe their guests, thus avoiding privacy issues.

Sometimes people notice things like fog, blackness, or "nothing." These are actually also guests that can be "sat with." Body pains, headaches and anything that comes when one starts to Focus is a "guest." If a pain comes, it is important to accept it and to hold it with no judgment or bias, even with kindness. Sometimes a participant will stop *Focusing* when a pain comes and then they keep that pain with them for the rest of the day. The fastest way to deal with such a pain is to return to the Guesthouse, invite the pain to be a guest, sit with it with kindness and listen to it.

Finally, it is important to remind participants during this activity of the need for confidentiality. Within the workshop, we generally talk about process, not content, meaning that we talk about what it is like to participate as Focuser or Listener. As I have indicated, the Focusers don't have to share any details of a past memory or event. But if they do, then the Companion or Listener does not tell others the details of what was said. Any personal information shared at the workshop remains in the workshop.

Handout 6A: Rumi Poem #1 "The Guest House"

This being human is a guest house.
Every morning a new arrival.

A joy, a depression, a meanness,
some momentary awareness comes
as an unexpected visitor.

Welcome and entertain them all!
Even if they're a crowd of sorrows,
who violently sweep your house
empty of its furniture,
still, treat each guest honourably.
He may be clearing you out
for some new delight.

The dark thought, the shame, the malice,
meet them at the door laughing,
and invite them in.

Be grateful for whoever comes,
because each has been sent
as a guide from beyond.

Jalaludin-e-Balkhi Rumi
Translated by
Coleman Barks

I am remembering that I am not alone and that the Divine is with me here, now.

I am taking time to be here in my Guesthouse. I am sensing my body, first the outer areas, then inside in my throat, chest, stomach...

I invite inner guests, whatever wants my attention now...

* * *

I'm noticing something...
I'm saying hello to this guest...
I'm finding the best way to describe how it is in my body...
I'm asking my listener for reflection when I want it.
I'm checking the words with my body...

* * *

I'm seeing if it's OK to just be with this guest...
I'm sitting by the guest with interest and kindness...
I'm sensing if it has a feeling or emotion...
I'm asking my listener for reflection when I want it.
I'm checking the words with my guest.
I'm letting it know I hear it...
I'm inviting my guest to let me know more...

* * *

I'm checking with my guest if it is OK to stop soon...
I'm letting it know I'm willing to come back...
I'm thanking my body, my guest, and Allah or God...
I'm coming out from the inside to be here now.

Handout 6C: Pat's Guide for the Companion

- Take a moment to remember that Allah (or the Divine Presence) is with us here, now.
- When it feels right, sense into your body, first the outer areas, then inside in your throat, chest, stomach... (As the Focuser goes inside, go to your Calm Safe Place, too)
- Next take time to be in your Calm Safe Place... (Pause here and give the Focuser a chance to go to her/his inner Calm Place and wait for them to tell you it's OK to move on)
- When you are ready, move into your Guest House... (Pause)
- You may invite inner guests to join you, whatever wants your attention now... (Pause)

* * *

- When you notice something you can let me know... (wait for the Focuser to speak and then reflect back what s/he says...)
- You might want to say Salam (or Hello) to this guest. (Pause and be aware of Presence in you. Wait until the Focuser indicates it is OK to say the next point...)
- Next, you might want to find the best way to describe how it is in your body... (Pause and reflect what the Focuser says. Wait until the Focuser lets you know it's OK to continue...)

* * *

- You may want to see if it's OK to just be with this guest... (Pause and wait after each invitation for the Focuser to let you know s/he is ready...)
- You might just want to sit by the guest with interest and kindness... (Pause)
- Maybe you can sense if it has a feeling or emotion... (Pause again and reflect what the Focuser says... then offer the next invitation)
- You might just want check the words with your guest... (Pause again and reflect what the Focuser says... then offer the next invitation)
- You can let it know you hear it... (Pause again and reflect what the Focuser says... then offer the next invitation)
- Maybe you can invite your guest to let you know more... (Pause again and reflect what the Focuser says... then repeat this invitation with pauses between each until the Focuser says his/her guest has no more to offer at this time)

* * *

- You might just want to check with your guest if it's OK to stop soon...(Pause ... then offer the next invitation)
- Maybe you can ask your guest what it wants for you, perhaps something that could be positive in your life... (Pause again and reflect what the Focuser says)
- If it feels right you can let your guest know you are willing to come back... (Pause and wait until the Focuser lets you know it's OK to continue)
- Take some time now to thank your body, your guest, and Allah (or the Divine Presence) ... (Pause while the Focuser does this)
- When it feels right, you can bring your awareness back to the room, taking a deep breath and opening your eyes.

7. PRESENCE

Although we didn't start our trainings this way, we quickly learned that Focusing taps a deep spiritual connection, and that this happens again and again in differing cultures. Although we did not mention the Divine, the participants quickly brought it in. When sensing inside, they often felt a "Presence."

You do not have to think of "Presence" as something spiritual. We usually teach "Presence" as a way of being with the "guests" you find inside. You might consider it an attitude that holds a space for anything that comes in a kind, compassionate way, without judgment and without having any goal to change or fix that thing. Being "in Presence with" something is to give gentle attention to it, to be curious and open to learning whatever that "something" or "guest" might need. Being in Presence is being a calm companion to whatever part of you needs attention.

Two Focusing teachers have created a useful entry into Presence. Barbara McGavin and Dr. Ann Weiser Cornell describe a state-of-being which they call "Self-in-Presence." "When our Self is in a state of Presence, we are capable of acting with flow, sensing the whole situation... connecting with the here-and-now, and interacting freely with our environment. We call this Self-in-Presence. [This] is not an object within ourselves that we have to find. As we look out of our eyes, as we act in the world: embodied, calm, appropriately friendly and curious, we could say we are Self-in-Presence. As we experience ourselves from the inside, as we sense the intricacy of our situations, as we create a safe inner environment for those aspects of our being that need rehabilitation, we could say we are Self-in-Presence." (FocusingResources.com "Treasure Maps to the Soul," 2008)

Surprisingly, a poem by Rumi mentions Presence by name.

> *This we have now is not imagination.*
> *This is not grief or joy.*
> *Not a judging state, nor an elation, nor sadness.*
> *Those come and go.*
> *This is the Presence that doesn't.*
>
> By Rumi
> Translated by
> Coleman Barks

In Islam, to hold something in Presence is to hold it with the help of God's grace and love. This is where we find ourselves as "the Lover in the presence of the Beloved." Afghans tell me that *Focusing* is very Sufi. One man told me that he had studied Sufism for years but never understood how to get to Presence before he worked with my colleague and me. Many Afghans relate that they now have a habit of Focusing alone, during prayer time.

In one area, where there were many Taliban fighters, the lead trainer who had supervised the psychosocial training program for AFSC was very nervous to continue the training. One man in her class was clearly pro-Taliban. She was unsure how he would react to *Focusing*. Then one day she returned to the office with exciting news. This man, whom she had feared, had stood up in class and said: "This is true Islam! Everyone should learn this *Focusing* and the Psychosocial Wellness program." He took the training to a local mosque, where he continued to give classes even after funding for the project had ended. *Community Wellness Focusing* in the mosque then continued over five years, and was well accepted in the community.

Sufi Muslims are not the only ones who feel comfortable with *Focusing*. The Japanese also have a tradition of inner sensing. Their language has a certain vagueness that demands that one sense the speaker's meaning. In other words, in order to understand what is being said, one has to be present with the other person, hold the whole situation and sense into it. Perhaps this is why *Focusing*, and now, *Community Wellness Focusing*, have spread readily in that country.

The Buddhist meditative tradition also fits well with *Focusing*. The meditator trains himself to have no judgments, no bias, and no desire to change anything. His goal, if he has one, is to have no goal, but to open the mind and free it from thought. This is also a form of Presence, although *Focusing* would add a bodily-awareness, an openness to feelings or images, and a special attentiveness to any shift in bodily-felt meaning. *Mindful Focusing*, developed by David Rome, describes this blend. It brings together Gendlin's felt-sense *Focusing* with Buddhist mindfulness-awareness practices, as described in his book: *Your Body Knows the Answer: Using Your Felt Sense to Solve Problems, Effect Change, and Liberate Creativity.*

In the Christian religious tradition, the concept of Presence is perhaps best described as the influence of the Holy Spirit. In the early 1970's, Peter A. Campbell and Edwin M. McMahon, Catholic priests and psychologists, "began to explore the link between *Focusing* and spirituality. They found that the body's ability to experience felt meaning revealed a hidden bridge into the experience of Spirit." (See "BioSpirituality" by Campbell and McMahon)

In 1975 they founded the *BioSpiritual Institute, Inc.*, a network of people from different ages and backgrounds who practice *BioSpiritual Focusing* in their daily lives. The Institute is not affiliated with any church, political party, country, or vested interest. The title of their second book sums up their approach: *Rediscovering the Lost Body-Connection Within Christian Spirituality: The Missing Link for Experiencing Yourself* (2011).

No matter what the culture, it seems we can all benefit from giving calm attention to our inner sensing, by being fully present with how we are experiencing a situation or problem. As we spend more time giving attention in this way, the surprising result is that we can often experience a "shift," or a new way of carrying the situation. Often we can sense what our next step could be, i.e, what action will move our life forward in a positive way. But more significant than finding a solution is that we discover a change in our relationship to the problem. This shift seems almost to come as a gift from outside us and can give us a profound sense of gratitude.

Our task, then, is to be open to all. Holding something in Presence—or being in Presence with our emotions, an issue, a problem that confronts us—is the essence of *Focusing*.

This is not easy, especially if emotions are high or a situation seems overwhelming. When this happens, and it seems difficult to come into Presence, we can notice whatever is getting in the way and be kind and gentle with *that.* Then automatically we are in Presence. We don't have to struggle against what is in the way in order to be Present. We just "stretch" and become bigger around whatever is blocking us. We sit gently with the "whole" of the situation, giving our attention to it all, including those parts that are fearful, overwhelmed or anxious.

For more information:

Reference to McGavin and Cornell's article "Treasure Maps to the Soul" can be found at:
>   http://www.focusingresources.com/ourlibrary/#articles

David Rome's meditative approach and his book can be found at:
>   www.mindfulfocusing.com (his website)

Campbell and McMahon's article "Biospiritual Focusing" can be found at:
>   http://www.focusing.org/biospirit.htm

Campbell and McMahon's website is:
>   www.biospiritual.org

Concerning Sufism and Presence see:

Living Presence (Revised): The Sufi Path to Mindfulness and the Essential Self by Kabir Helminski. Random House, New York, NY, 2017

Activity 7A: Defining Presence

Goals: To introduce Presence and help participants get an initial feel for the concept and how it applies to their lives.

Materials: Paper and pencils. Copies of Handout 7A if you want to use it. Invite participants to bring their journals to class.

Time: 20 minutes

* * *

Explain: Presence is a state of holding something with:

- No judgment
- No goals or agenda
- No bias or preference
- No desire to change or control your own feelings or anyone else's

It can be described as holding something (self, a part of self, or others) with *kindness*. We found that Presence and Presence language is crucial to *Focusing*, and crucial to working with any group wishing for psychosocial wellness. Presence helps us find just the right amount of distance from our guests, and allows us to hold what comes in a compassionate way.

Sensing: Take a moment to feel what it is like to be accepted with kindness and without judgment. Maybe it is when someone listened to you and did not judge you in any way. Instead, they accepted you just as you were at that moment, regardless of what you said.

Write it down: What did that feel like? Try to capture the words or phrases that fit your experience.

Share: Now take a moment to share this description with someone sitting close to you in the group. Feel free to write more if something comes up.

Discussion: Invite sharing with the whole group as people feel comfortable. Especially note which aspects of Presence the participants have in common.

Activity 7B: Finding a Place of Gratitude

<u>Goals:</u> To experience Presence through a feeling of gratitude.

<u>Materials:</u> Handout 7A (optional)

<u>Time:</u> 20-30 minutes

* * *

Read aloud to the group, the poem by Rumi called "This We Have Now" (Handout 7A at end of this chapter). Ask them to note that emotions, whether pleasant or painful, are not here to stay.

Ask for comments on Presence in this poem, such as:

- Presence is permanent, but it has to be nurtured. You can practice being in Presence with positive situations and emotions so that you can be ready to use it with difficult ones.

- It is the attitude of kindness and "just being with" something in yourself or in someone else.

- When in Presence, you are whole and calm.

- In Presence you sense and nurture your own inner states and those of others.

Practice: Find Presence with the group by inviting everyone to think of something in their lives they are grateful for. It does not matter if it is something very small.

- Ask the group to relax and lead them back into their Calm Safe Place.

- Invite them to bring that sense of calmness and safety around the *'something grateful'.*

95

- Sense where the gratitude is in your body.

- Sense how your body feels with this gratitude.

- As you bring your attention back to the room, bring that feeling with you.

Discussion: How was this exercise for you? Who would like to share what happened?

- Discuss problems anyone may have had being in Presence with this place of gratitude. Remind them that, if they know they are not there, that is a sign that their body is helping. 'It' (a guest or part-of-self) is telling them that "Now is not the time." And that is good to know.

- Are you able to come into Presence?

- Is checking inside easy or difficult?

Note to trainer: Before teaching this module, practice introducing Presence to your friends and family so that you are comfortable leading a group. Use art, poetry or other ways to help the learning process.

When you talk about Presence to the workshop, you can describe how it feels in you, i.e, some of the qualities it carries. However, make clear that this is your own personal way of holding Presence. Each person has an individual way of feeling Presence, although there are common points that you can help them locate.

It is important that the group feels safe and comfortable when giving their input. Encourage people to share only what feels right and of course not to share at all if they prefer. Facilitate the discussions by modeling Presence for each person as they talk. Remember to ask each person if there is anything more that comes.

If you start talking about Presence early in your workshops, people will see it as an integral part of the *Focusing* process. In a short workshop, I often put this module about gratitude at the beginning.

Activity 7C: How Presence Fits Your Culture

Discuss: Talk about how Presence is found throughout the world in many different outward forms but the inner attitude is the same—of kindly holding the space without judging or trying to control.

Ask where they can find examples of Presence that come from their own culture and way of life. What expresses compassionate kindness in your community?

Let them write, then share with the group: maybe a Poem or Poet, a Religious Text, or a Symbol. Start a collection of these by writing them on cards or flipcharts and placing them on the walls around the room.

Homework: How can you share these things with those you live with or with friends? As homework, can you share the concept of Presence with someone in your life? Also notice when you find yourself holding something in Presence. Make a note of those times in your journal, and/or share it with us the next time we meet.

Handout 7A: Rumi Poem #2 "This We Have Now"

> *This we have now is not imagination.*
> *This is not grief or joy.*
> *Not a judging state, nor an elation, nor sadness*
> *Those come and go.*
> *This is the presence that doesn't.*
>
> By Rumi
> Translated by
> Coleman Barks

8: GOOD LISTENING/THE STORYTELLER

When I was working in Liberia for WHO (the World Health Organization) as their medical anthropologist, I did a lot of listening to others. But in order to be effective in listening to other people, I needed my needs to be listened to also. A plague like Ebola is worse than a war. In war, you hear the rockets and you sense the direction danger might come from. When working with an infectious disease, you can never be sure you are safe; you are not even sure where the danger lies. Although we knew Ebola was spread only by contact with body fluids, we did not know how long the virus could survive on damp surfaces.

It was also extremely important for us not to get sick in any other way. Can you imagine coming down with the flu in a situation where every fever and stomach problem could be blamed, rightly or wrongly, on Ebola? What if I got a gastro-intestinal infection, common in a developing country, or if I caught malaria, which was in season? I might then be quarantined with Ebola sufferers. It is easy to become over concerned—can I say obsessed?—by such fears.

When I first arrived, the disease was spiraling out of control. While attending a government Ebola Task Force meeting, I noticed everyone in the room was scared and they were fighting over small issues. I went back to the hotel in fear for my life. I sat in my room in shock, trying to process what I had heard. I thought: "Oh Pat! What on earth did you get yourself into this time? How can you possibly stay safe enough to get home?"

I sat at my desk in that small, dark, hotel room, holding my head in hands, tears streaming down my face. I stared at my computer. Because Liberia is in the same time zone as the UK, I realized I could contact some *Focusing* friends and find someone to listen to me so I could sort out my turbulent feelings. I found several people awake at that time and they were able to provide me with a *Focusing* Presence. Others wrote to me later to let me know I could disturb them anytime. That outpouring of support was critical to me and gave me the strength to face my fears and continue my work.

I tell this story to show that psychosocial wellness is as critical to health workers as it is to beleaguered citizens. It is also to show that psychosocial wellness is as important as physical wellness in being able to meet life's challenges. The good news is that psychological support can be found anytime, anywhere, through *Focusing*. If I hadn't found a listening companion, I would have eventually found the strength inside me on my own. But having a friend or colleague sit with me, even just over the internet, eased my struggle and made the Ebola challenge easier to bear.

It also made me sensitive to the needs of other aide workers. I would often drop by their office, sit on the edge of their desk, and suggest they close their eyes and take a mini-break, imagining themselves in a calm, safe place. Sometimes a caring and empathetic presence is the greatest gift we can offer each other. Even in the most harrowing of events, having someone listen to you brings an incredible amount of healing. So being able to listen to another person without judgment, without taking sides, without even a goal, is a great gift to give another person, and a gift I appreciated deeply in Liberia at that time.

Kathleen Dowling Singh, a dharma teacher who supports people through the dying process, has written, "The gift of our complete and focused attention is one of the kindest gifts we can give each other." ("The Gift of Attention" by K.D. Singh, in *The Wisdom of Listening,* Brady, M. [ed], Wisdom Publishing, MA, 2003)

Focusing Founder Gene Gendlin said, "The essence of working with another person is to be present as a living being. And that is lucky, because if we had to be smart, or good, or mature, or wise, then we would probably be in trouble. But what matters is not that. What matters is to be a human being with another human being, to recognize the other person as another being in there." (Eugene Gendlin, Leuven Conference, 1989)

It turns out that listening to the concerns of the citizens and health aides was one of my main contributions during the Ebola crisis in 2014-15. Anthropologists are trained to listen to people and to try to understand their point of view. The good news is that anyone who wants to, can do it.

So it is not too surprising that my research methodology relied largely on empathic listening. I and my team of local researchers met with people who were frustrated and scared. We would say, "We are from the World Health Organization (WHO) and we want to hear what you want us to know about Ebola. Because what you say is important, we have a team to make sure we hear everything you say. We will write down whatever you need to tell us about Ebola and what is happening in your community." This was done with no judgment and no desire to hear anything in particular. Because of this openness and empathy, people had much to say.

The process of interviewing a group of people was like the five "steps" of a *Focusing* session:

1. We entered and said hello.

2. We invited whatever wanted to be heard.

3. We reflected back what was said, to show we were really hearing what people had to say.

4. We asked if there was anything more that needed to be said.

5. We thanked them for sharing.

As they felt heard, we could feel a shift in their collective attitudes and knew there was some relief for their troubled feelings. When we returned to a community later in the month, we often found these same communities engaged in positive self-help and community care.

I include one more story about listening, this time from Pakistan. Wajid is a *Focusing* Trainer with a background in social work. He integrates *Focusing* frequently into daily interactions. He shared with me the following story, which he calls the "The Kissa-Khani Story Listeners."

> Last week I traveled to Narran. On the way back we had to stop for a couple of hours due to a landslide on the highway, near where the wilderness leads to the Kissa-Khani Bazaar which means the Bazaar of the Story Tellers. Drivers and passengers from all over Pakistan were standing around and chatting to each other. They were all stressed, not so much because of the roadblock, but because of the overall tension in which we live.
>
> Everyone was talking, but not listening to the others. I asked three men to walk across the landslide with me and see what was happening on the other side. The purpose of the walk was to take them away from the crowd and to limit the number of people I would interact with. While walking across and then back, I made sure we listened to each other with empathy. One

was a professional from the hospitality industry, another a landowner from Punjab, and the third a Jeep driver from Narran. Since we had such diverse backgrounds, I suggested we give ourselves a chance to listen to each other, as we would not get such a chance again. As strangers, we could tell each other things we cannot tell those we know. Still, I said, we should tell only what we're comfortable with.

It was a great experience. I utilized several Community Wellness exercises, including story-telling and much listening. Those few hours together changed their mood and how they looked at life. When parting, they asked me who I was, and I told them, "You must have heard of the Kissa-Khani story-tellers?" They said yes. I said, "I am the Kissa-Khani story *listener*. I believe that we need more story listeners than tellers. Maybe we should call our little group the "Kissa-Khani story *listeners*.

Activity 8A: Qualities of Good Listening

<u>Goals:</u> By the end of this module, participants will have explored the qualities of good listening, and have practiced listening with another person. By learning to listen well to another person, they learn the role of being a true companion. As they get better at listening to others, they get better at listening to themselves.

<u>Materials:</u> Flipchart and markers

<u>Time:</u> 30 minutes

* * *

Remembering:

Suggest to the group that they...

- Sit back, take a deep breath and slowly blow it out. Let your awareness come into your body...your arms and hands...your legs and feet...and the contact of your body on what you're sitting on... now let your awareness come inward, into the inner area of your body, throat, chest, stomach, belly...

- Now think of a time when you were fully listened to. Sense what that felt like in your body. Notice how it feels now as you bring that memory into your body. Take your time to invite or sense what image, felt sense or words come with this memory.

- As you hold this awareness, notice what the person said or did to let you know they really, deeply heard you. Sense how your body feels as you recall this event. Notice where you carry this feeling in your body. Maybe find a gesture, word, phrase or image to describe that.

- And now, take another moment to sense what you want to share about this experience.

- When you are ready, bring your attention back to the room.

105

Discussion:

- If the group is new to Focusing, ask if they felt comfortable with the exercise, and if they got a felt sense.
- Ask if anyone would like to describe the felt sense of their memories.
- When a quality of a good listener is described, write that on the flipchart.

Remembering again:

Repeat the earlier remembering, only this time ask them to sense into a memory of an occasion when they listened to someone else fully. Invite them to sense how that felt in their body and to take time to detect what image, felt sense or words come with this memory.

Discussion again:

- Ask for volunteers to describe the felt sense of their memories.
- When a quality of a good listener is described, add that to the flipchart.

Define Listening: Explain that good listening varies from culture to culture, so each group needs to define it for themselves. Ask:

- How do *you* define good listening?
- What are the signs that someone is truly listening to you?
- How do you know if someone is *not* listening to you?
- Are there any local sayings or adages that convey good listening in your community?

Encourage descriptions, gestures, words and phrases. Record what is said on the flipchart and place the list on display so that these qualities can be referred to later. Invite participants to add to the list as more ideas come.

Some qualities which might be on the list are:

- Listening is hearing what someone tells you.
- Listening is holding a space for someone, so that they can say their thoughts and feelings.
- Listening is when you hear but do not try to fix or solve the problem.
- It is not passive, but active and interested, paying attention.
- Eye contact (but this can vary in different cultures).
- Avoiding, or coming right back from, distractions.
- Listening kindly.
- Being patient.
- Sensing non-verbal messages.
- Not giving advice or criticism.
- Maybe making a sound or nodding.

In addition, be sure to list ways that each participant can let someone know he or she is listening. Use another page of the flipchart if needed, or have them make their own list. You may want to ask the group how these ways of listening vary by age and gender.

You can also brainstorm the qualities of a good listener. Ask each person in the room to contribute a quality. (Brainstorming is described in Chapter 11, and in Handout 11A)

If there is time, have participants contrast good and bad listening through a ten-minute Role Play. Use Activity 9C in Chapter 9.

Note to trainer: Be sure to model the qualities of good listening while the group gives feedback. Some people may say that they have never felt listened to, or that they have never really listened to anyone. If this happens, be sure to make time to reflect this sharing. You might offer a gentle suggestion that they imagine what it *might* be like to be really heard, even if it has never happened to them, and to sense in their body how that might feel.

Since the definition of good listening varies according to culture, there is no single way to define it. For example, many books in Western culture note that eye contact is important, yet other parts of the world consider it rude (such as a young person staring at an elder) or sexually suggestive (such as eye contact between a man and a woman). Each culture has its own way of showing someone they are listening. You as trainer may know the culture, but allow the group to explore this for themselves.

You might also have them consider how people actually listen in their community. Do people really listen, or do they tend to jump in with advice? Bring the group's awareness to this. For additional insights, make a list of key points from the group when they answer the question:

- Who listens?
- How do they listen?

Activity 8B: The Storyteller (Deep Listening)

<u>Goals:</u> At the end of this activity, participants will have experienced deep listening and shared a story with someone else in the group.

<u>Materials:</u> Handouts 8A and 8B for each person (optional)

<u>Time:</u> Approximately 45 minutes (30 minutes for the storytelling activity; 15 for the discussion)

* * *

Storytelling:

Distribute Handouts 8A and 8B if you have them.

Invite participants to think about a story in their lives. It should be something personal that has a slight emotional content. Ask them to do the following:

- Check inside to see if you are comfortable sharing this story. If not, select another.
- Choose a partner with whom you will share stories, possibly someone who does not know you very well.
- Since everyone in the room does this exercise at the same time, each pair needs to find a physical place where they will feel relatively secluded.
- One partner will be the first storyteller, and then you will switch. Check inside to see which of you wants to go first.
- As you relate your story, give yourself time to:
  - Go inside to sense what is OK to say.
  - Notice any feelings you have about this story.
  - Share how you feel about it in your body.
- Before finishing the story, see if there is anything else that wants to be said.

109

If you are listening to the story, *do not say anything.* Instead:

- Bring your awareness into your body. Come to that place that is calm, safe and beautiful.

- Next, include the storyteller in your awareness, as if you were sitting in your safe place with the storyteller.

- Be calm, patient, interested.

- You may show your interest in the story without talking. You can say: "um... uh huh..." or other culturally appropriate sounds. You can nod, smile, and use facial expressions.

- It is helpful if you time the story (suggestion: 10-15 minutes each) and let the storyteller know when he or she has only 5 minutes left.

Trade places and repeat.

Discussion:

- What did it feel like as the *storyteller*?
- What did it feel like to be listened to?
- What did listening in this way feel like as the *companion*?
- Was it difficult to listen without talking? Why or why not?

Homework assignment:

At home tonight, spend time with one person in your household and completely listen to that person for 10 minutes. Do not tell them in advance what you are doing or why. Just sense how it feels to listen in this way. Talk about the activity afterwards, explaining what you did. Ask them how they felt as you listened to them with deep attention.

I have found that children especially are often thrilled to have such undivided and uncritical time from a parent.

Note to trainer: As you facilitate this activity, keep in mind that it is natural for people to want to help the person who is talking, often by giving advice. For a novice *Focusing* companion, we have found that when we restrict any talking, the companion starts afresh, just listening. It is a contrived situation but it illustrates something important—which is that the most important part of being a companion is to be present.

You will probably need to remind them in subsequent *Focusing* activities to use the same calm, patient Presence. If you can remember what it was like for you the first time you did it, you can use your understanding to shape your group's experience. And of course, you, the facilitator, need to model this kind of deep listening for the participants at every opportunity.

Handout 8A: The Storyteller

I'm bringing my awareness into my body…
Starting with my feet…
Then my legs…
Back…
Arms, shoulders…
Head…
And into my center.

I'm thinking of the story I want to tell…
I check inside to sense what is OK with me to talk about…
I notice any feelings inside me about this story.

I take time to tell the event and sense how my body feels about it…
Before finishing the story, I see if there is anything else that wants
to be said…

After telling the story,
I sense what it felt like to be listened to by my companion…
I check to see if I feel any different now than before I told the story.

Handout 8B: The Companion to the Storyteller

Ask the Storyteller:
- "How is this distance between us?"
- "How many minutes of warning would you like before your time is up?"
- Be sure to time the story (10-15 min).

Now in silence...
- Bring your awareness into your own body for a short time.
- Come to that place in you that is calm, safe and beautiful.

Then bring your awareness back to the Storyteller:
- As if you were still sitting in the safe place with the Storyteller.
- Be gentle, calm and patient.
- Show your interest with murmurs and nods and facial expressions if you wish.
- Listen and be with the Storyteller.

When time is almost over, say:
- "We have about __ more minutes."

After listening to the story, notice:
- What it was like to listen without helping.
- Where it might have been difficult to stay with the Storyteller.
- What you sense in your body at this time.

9. STRESS AND EMOTIONS

People who have been through traumatic events find it useful to learn about stress and emotions. The activities in this chapter are not unique to *Community Wellness Focusing*, and many mental health programs teach the same basic information. But it is always useful to review what is normal and what is not in this area; what is culturally accepted and what is not. It is also useful to know that stress can bring out "abnormal" or culturally unacceptable emotions.

From my very first Focusing workshop, I discovered that *Focusing* relieves stress. In comments after that workshop, one aide worker stated, "Old family issues and pain about the [Afghan] war were weighing me down, always increasing my tension and anger. Now those things are much better." Another man looked at me with amazement.

Having had a stress-related pain in his side for a long time, he was surprised to find that it left after he focused on it. All the staff who attended this workshop agreed that *Focusing* helped them feel hopeful and more relaxed despite the worry and uncertainty of their country's situation.

Living in the crowded Gaza Strip is very stressful; civilians have suffered 60 years of war, occupation and blockade. The Palestinian Trauma Centre (PTC), organized in 2007 by a Palestinian psychologist, Dr. Mohamed Altawil, reports on his website that "approximately 700,000 Palestinians (children and adults) urgently need psychological, social and medical help. Children are suffering from severe psychological, social and behavioral disorders as a result of constant exposure to the traumas produced by the ongoing war, occupation and blockade."

Focusing was unknown in Gaza in 2007. However, Mohamed Altawil discovered the technique when he came to England to pursue his psychological studies. He felt it would help the children who came to the PTC. He invited a team of Focusers to help him develop a program which could teach *Focusing* to his staff. The team consisted of Mohamed, and Focusers from England, Ireland, and the Netherlands (Jerry Conway, Mary Jennings, Lina Geha, Simon Kilner, and, later, René Veugelers.)

Getting permission for the team to enter Gaza presented some difficult political challenges, as well as teaching questions. How much *Focusing* could be taught in four days? How much time *should* it take? Could Europeans teach *Focusing* in the Arab culture? Would aide workers at the PTC be receptive to this "Western" method?

In the end, with funding from the Irish Quakers (IQFA), British Quakers and The International Focusing Institute, the team was able to teach two four-day workshops, one in 2011 and one in 2013, supported during the interval by materials that Mohamed translated into Arabic and also by many Skype calls. Mohamed developed pre- and post-assessment tools and found that indeed *Focusing* lowered stress. Encouraged by this finding, he took *Focusing* further. One of the team, Ghada Radwan, really understood how *Focusing* could help the people and became the project leader for *Focusing* with PTC. She trained a team of volunteers and staff and between them, they have now trained over 1,700 people.

It is wonderful for a culture to develop its own workbook for Community Wellness. Before that happens however, a transition can be gradually made from one culture to another. For instance, Jerry Conway, one of the Focusing team, knew my *Community Wellness Focusing* as it had been adapted to the Afghans. He had spent twelve weeks in Afghanistan with me in 2005 and had helped develop their Dari workbook. He shared some of the skills he knew with the Palestinians and the participants chose the ones that spoke to them. Some ideas were tried and rejected, and other ideas expanded. Activities were adapted to create a program that is their own, one that is culturally relevant and works in their situation.

For example, the Arabic culture in Gaza, which includes Sunni Muslims, does not embrace the Sufi or mystic side of Islam. So rather than Rumi's poetry, the Palestinians chose quotations from the Quran or Hadith to introduce this inner work. They used sayings that resonated with them or touched some inner feeling.

The idea of "guests" could not be introduced by a Rumi poem. Instead, the presenters performed a skit, in which one played the role of "participant" and another played the role of "a feeling." The "participant" met the "feeling", invited it to sit down at a café, then asked what it wanted to say, and so on through the five stages of *Focusing*, ending with a thank-you and good-bye. (See Chapter 8, p. 98 for the five steps of a Focusing session.)

Participants had trouble touching personal feelings. They had been forced to ignore them in order to survive. They needed time to understand the difference between feeling and thinking, so this subject was frequently discussed. Holding an object helped them to feel, particularly if it held some personal symbolic meaning, such as a key or a teddy bear. Bending a dry stick, then a green stick (Activity 9A) helped them successfully internalize the difference between bending and breaking so this sensory exercise was expanded to include all participants.

Jerry Conway notes, "The joy of *Focusing* is that it's a self-help process, which is important in an area where you haven't much access to psychosocial services. It's a way people can keep themselves well and develop their resilience. The particular finding in Gaza is that when you live with major trauma, it's difficult to sense into feelings. You can't go directly to them ... *Community Wellness Focusing* enables people to touch into feelings without getting overwhelmed, in a safe way."

For more information:
About the Palestinian Trauma Centre:
       http://en.ptcgaza.com/
       http://www.ptcuk.org/
For a video by the Palestinian Trauma Centre about Focusing in Gaza (10 minutes long with English subtitles):
       https://www.youtube.com/watch?v=Vu6mUJb9TCk&feature=youtu.be

Activity 9A: Dry Stick, Green Stick

Note: This Activity could come at any point in your workshop, perhaps after the Introduction (Chapter 2), or as a lead into Stories of Resilience (Chapter 5.) Here, it is used as a quick way to explain "Resilience" to a group, before leading them into other activities.

Goal: By the end of the module, participants will:

1. Identify resiliency skills which they and their community already have
2. Recognize immediate and long-term stress responses in themselves and others.

Materials: For a demonstration, one dry stick (be sure you have one that will break after 3 or 4 bending pressures); one green stick (one that won't break no matter how much it is bent, but will spring back to near normal shape); a flipchart or drawing surface, and something to write with. For everyone to have the experience (see Variation), you will need as many green and dry sticks as participants, plus a few extra in case some sticks prove unsuitable.

Time: 20-30 minutes

* * *

Object Lesson: Hold a dry stick by the ends and bend it a little more for every stress which the people name that has happened in their community. After three or four times, it will break. Tell the group, "This is something like what happens to people who are overcome by stress. How do you know when someone in your community is overcome by stress?" Collect some examples of stress reactions they have seen recently.

119

Now hold the green stick by the ends and have the people name the stressors again, while you bend the stick a bit each time. After the list is done, let go of one end of the stick and let everyone see the stick spring back straight.

Say to the group, "Resiliency is the ability to keep going when things get bad. You people are wonderfully resilient. You find many effective ways to deal with stress every day."

Variation: Activities must be adapted to different cultures and circumstances, so variations are encouraged. In Gaza, participants found it helpful to let everyone in the group have both a dry stick and a green stick. In this way, each person received the physical sensation of breaking the one and bending the other. When people feel the sensation in their bodies, they better remember and integrate the message into their lives.

Small Group Discussion: Divide the large group into small groups for 10 minutes or so, and ask each group to write a list of things they have noticed in their community that help people stay healthy and cope in difficult times. Then have them come back to the group and make a master list. Below are some items to add if people don't find something like them. Participants may want to copy the group list to take home, in order to remind themselves of these skills.

Sample list of things that help people cope in hard times

- Have a goal.

- Find resources, think creatively.

- Talk to family and friends.

- Help others.

- Show kindness to others.

- Remember good things.

- Have a vision of things getting better.

- Have positive and negative feelings without getting overwhelmed.

- Have faith in a divine power.

Note to trainer: By discussing positive examples of when they were resilient, people discover that they already have resources inside that have helped them. People may also share times when it has been hard to be resilient. Listen to these examples with compassion and kindness.

Activity 9B: Normal Stress Reactions

<u>Goals:</u> By the end of this activity, participants will be able to identify normal stress reactions and discuss the effects of prolonged stress on people's emotions, physical wellbeing and behavior. This activity will help people understand that their stress reactions are OK and that all human beings share them. Often just knowing that reactions are shared can alleviate stress.

<u>Materials:</u> Flipcharts, paper, markers, tape, Handout 9A at the end of the chapter (to be distributed after the lecture is completed)

<u>Time:</u> 40 minutes

* * *

A. Discussion: Begin with a series of questions.

- How many of you, or someone in your family, suffer from headaches?
- How many of you, or someone in your family, suffer from sleep problems? Maybe you cannot fall asleep, or you fall asleep but wake after a few hours and cannot go back to sleep.
- How many of you, or someone in your family, suffer from stomach aches, or stomach problems?
- How many of you, or someone in your family, suffer from generalized body pains?
- How many of you, or someone in your family, suffer from heart problems like high blood pressure or heart disease?
- How many of you, or someone in your family, regularly take pills for pain, stress or sleep?

Many in the group will raise their hands or indicate they have these problems. Highlight how common these symptoms are and discuss how these complaints are common signs of stress.

B: Presentation: How the body reacts to stress.

Tell them that stress is a normal part of life. Without stress the body and mind would atrophy. Astronauts in space are weightless; this condition is a challenge to the health of their bones and muscles. Some stress or weight is required for our wellbeing.

Healthy reactions to stress:

- Fight—defend self against danger
- Flight—leave area of danger
- Freeze—hide from danger

Stress can have a positive outcome if there is:

- A return to one's prior status
- Increased adaptability

Stress has a negative outcome if it results in:

- Emotional Disturbance
- Physical illness
- Psychosomatic illness

Initial physical symptoms of stress are:

- Increased heart rate
- Increased blood volume
- Elevated blood pressure
- Cold hands and feet as blood is directed away from extremities and digestive system into the larger muscles that can help you fight or run
- Dilated pupils (sharpened vision)
- More acute hearing

Possible long-term reactions:

- Impaired digestion
- Slowed growth and tissue repair
- Immune system problems that cause sickness
- Inflammatory responses that cause aches and pain

Effects of Stress

- Environment: "How are you affected by your surroundings? In what ways does your behavior change when you are experiencing stress?"
- Body: "How is your body affected? What changes happen in your body?"
- Thoughts/Emotions: "How does stress affect the way you perceive situations or problems? What emotions do you feel?"

Note to trainer: When presenting the material you can break up the "lecture" style a bit by beginning each section by asking about their experience. For example, you might ask what they know to be a positive stress reaction. Do they have any examples, in themselves or others? What would be a negative reaction? Again, examples?

After the presentation, distribute Handout 9A on Stress Outcomes located at the end of this chapter. Or make a visual chart of the information and go through the list with the group, reviewing the many effects stress has on our behavior, our body, our emotions, or our thoughts. I suggest the chart or Handout come after your discussion, so that they listen to the presentation with a fresh mind. (See additional Note to Trainer on page 122)

C: Discussion on cultural reactions to stress:

Make the following points with the whole group:

- What is considered stressful varies from culture to culture.
- How people cope with stress is also culturally defined.
- Stress is an interaction between culture, environment and individual personalities.

Divide the participants into small groups of 3 to 5 people. Supply each group with paper and markers, and give them the following assignment:

- Group 1 will discuss and list:
  - *Male* emotional reactions to stress
  - *Male* behavioral reactions to stress
- Group 2 will discuss and list:
  - *Female* emotional reactions to stress
  - *Female* behavioral reactions to stress

- Group 3 will discuss and list:
  - *Elderly* emotional reactions to stress
  - *Elderly* behavioral reactions to stress
- Group 4 will discuss and list:
  - *Children's* emotional reactions to stress
  - *Children's* behavioral reactions to stress

After the groups have completed the small group activities, have them post their lists on the walls and a spokesperson from each group can present their findings.

At the end of the presentations, note the common aspects of stress. Also, highlight how this awareness of common reactions can help participants know when someone in their family or community is in need of psychosocial support. Any changes in behavior can be an indication of trauma. Encourage them to contribute instances they have noticed in the community.

Note to trainer: You will find that in many countries, the symptoms of stress are not understood, and it is a great relief for your participants to find that their rapid heart beat or insomnia are considered "normal" stress reactions.

The truth is that there are no "abnormal" stress reactions. First of all, reactions vary widely from individual to individual. In addition, every reaction and every emotion serve a purpose, at least initially.

This would be a good time to review Handout 3A from Chapter 3 called "Defining Normal." This shows that normalcy is highly variable in individuals and cultures. For instance, some cultures value high emotional control, but others, high emotional expressiveness. What are the norms in your target culture?

Activity 9C: Role Play

Goals: To experience the stress relief that comes from "Emotional First Aid" or, in other words, Focusing-type listening.

Materials: None

Time: 20 minutes, plus 10 minutes per pair or triad.

* * *

Prepare: Divide the group into pairs or triads and label each person A, B, or C. Person A has the role of a person with a problem; person B is the listener, and person C (optional) can monitor the time and act as coach. Give 5 or 10 minutes for each group to decide on a hypothetical problem.

Have them perform for 5-6 minutes *without any prior practice.* They will ad-lib their lines, i.e. make them up on the spot. The plot, however, is the same for everyone. At first, the listener, Person B, will do a poor job of listening. Halfway through, the person with the problem, Person A, will say, "You're not listening!" This is the cue for Person B to change and start listening well, doing the Focusing-type listening as explained in the previous chapter.

Discussion: After each role play, highlight what has been done to represent poor listening, and what has been done to represent good listening. Emphasize ways in which listening relieves stress, but don't make each discussion too long; let the role-plays mostly speak for themselves.

At the end of all the presentations, open up the discussion for general comments.

128

Handout 9A: Stress Outcome

How does stress affect us? The initial reactions to stress include:
- Heart rate increases
- Blood volume increases
- Blood pressure increases
- Hands and feet get cold as blood is directed away from extremities and the digestive system into the larger muscles that can help you to fight or run
- Pupil dilate to sharpen vision
- Hearing becomes more acute

If stress continues these reactions remain and can adversely affect our:
- Behavior
  - Insomnia, nightmares, and other sleep problems.
  - Fatigue
  - Nervous tics, such as wringing hands
  - Hyperventilation
  - Inability to relax, pacing, fidgeting and restlessness
  - Crying
  - Weight gain or sudden weight loss
  - Loss of effectiveness at work
  - Recklessness
  - Increased smoking or drug use or gambling
- Body
  - Hyper-arousal
  - Hypertension
  - Headaches
  - Muscle spasms and aching shoulders neck and back
  - Indigestion and or nausea
  - Dry mouth
  - Shortness of breath
  - Heart palpitations
  - Cold hands and feet
  - Body aches
- Thoughts / Emotions
  - Shock, terror, anger
  - Guilt
  - Disbelief
  - Grief
  - Irritability
  - Helplessness
  - Regression to earlier developmental phase
  - Confusion or distortion
  - Self-blame
  - Intrusive thoughts
  - Decreased self-esteem/efficacy
  - Impaired concentration

10. Finding Inner Balance

Participants gain inner balance when they face difficult emotions through *Focusing*. The activities in this chapter encourage inner balance but they are not designed to be therapy. *Focusing* does not promote people talking about their problems. Rather, it uses the techniques of positive psychology to heighten awareness of personal resources.

Dr. Chris Peterson, one of the founders and leaders of positive psychology, explains that this branch of psychology consists of the scientific study of what makes life worth living. It calls for psychological science to be concerned with strength as well as weakness and to be interested in building the best things in life as well as repairing the worst. The techniques of positive psychology are tested and validated through the use of scientific method. One of the main discoveries is that "the good life" can be taught.

Does positive psychology say anything about our emotions, especially the problematic ones? Seven to fifteen basic emotions have been categorized by science. Apparently we combine these to create many subtle variations of emotional experience. Any attempt to eliminate negative emotions may have the unintended consequence of limiting the variety and subtlety of our experiences. Although efforts to increase positive emotions can cause the negative ones to fade in importance, it is not a good idea to suppress them. Suppressing our negative emotions also suppresses our positive ones. What we are looking for is a balance between the two.

Positive psychology looks for the positive value of each emotion, so I teach that no emotion is truly negative. Thank God we have fear and anger! Such reactions are there for a reason. But regardless of my topic, I end each class on a positive note. I want participants to return to their lives remembering what they are doing *right,* even in the face of problems, poverty, disasters, or warfare. I ask them what keeps them emotionally healthy and whether their social connections are working for them. By these two markers, they identify some traits that affect their psychosocial wellness—both positively and negatively—but we always return at the end of each discussion to the positive.

The following American Indian story called "Two Wolves" illustrates this balance.

> An old Cherokee was teaching his grandson about life. "A fight is going on inside me," he said to the boy. "It is a terrible fight and it is between two wolves. One is evil—he is anger, envy, sorrow, regret, greed, arrogance, self-pity, guilt, resentment, inferiority, lies, false pride, superiority, and ego. The other is good—he is joy, peace, love, hope, serenity, humility, kindness, benevolence, empathy, generosity, truth, compassion, and faith. The same fight is going on inside you—and inside every other person, too."
>
> The Grandson thought about it for a minute and then asked his grandfather, "Which wolf will win?" The old Cherokee simply replied, "Whichever one I feed."

As we practice positive psychology and move forward with *Focusing*, we learn that anger and some of these so-called 'bad' emotions are there to bring our awareness to something important. We can learn from negative feelings but we don't have to feed them. We can make the effort each day to remember the good things in our lives.

During my three-week visit to Chacala, Mexico, I was asked to teach some aspects of community resilience in a one-evening session. Mexico, according to research at the Hofstede Center, scores high on power distance (See Mexico's scores at http://geert-hofstede.com/mexico.html) "Power distance" means that inequalities of powers are expected and subordinates are accustomed to being told what to do. This perhaps explains why my brief work there, encouraging them to trust their own inner knowledge, was welcomed as remarkably helpful.

Prior to my one-evening session, we were asked to observe the privately-run afterschool program. The director explained the kids were always tired. They had been to school with teachers who were pretty violent, who never listened. There were issues at home too. All in all, the children were a needy, difficult group.

The director and myself, along with five Mexican Focusers and the program psychologist spent Monday afternoon at the program. Two of the Focusers resonated with the problems and wanted to visit again, but three of them found the situation very distressing. One woman actually went home.

It was clear that the afterschool teachers, hired to help with homework, didn't know about child development or how to help children suffering from violence in the home and community. They either ignored or yelled at children who were acting inappropriately. The competent program psychologist came twice a week, but she was overwhelmed. The children acted out in so many ways, such as isolating themselves or becoming violent. Some were begging for help in the way kids do, often by refusing help, or hitting other children, or running out of the compound and hiding from everyone.

The eight of us designed an evening program to use with the parents and teachers. Our *Focusing* team decided that we could best support positive parenting by having everyone get a felt-sense, or inner body knowing, of what it was like when they had been educated with fear, and how that felt different from when they had been educated with love. We used the concept of education for two reasons: 1) we were supporting an afterschool program, and 2) the use of the word "discipline" might have been seen as criticism of their parenting and we wanted to stay positive.

That Wednesday evening, we had a good turnout of 28 adults, including three men. Two Mexican Focusers conducted the class. First, they asked everyone to quiet down and close their eyes, and to notice in their body what it felt like as they recalled being educated with fear. None of the participants knew Focusing. There was some waiting, some prompts to check inside their body to see where they held that fear. "What comes for you?" they were asked. Then they talked about their inner felt sense and the memory that produced it. They shared quite easily in the large group, with comments like, "It was ugly, it made me feel stupid."

"Now close your eyes and bring in what it was like to be educated with love. Who did it, and how did it feel?" I could see a difference in their bodies. I could see smiles and relaxing faces. Then they said things like, "I felt expansive, I felt warmth, I felt caring." They discussed educating their own kids with love and gave examples of that. "I made him a special meal to show I cared," etc.

After this, they broke into small groups of five, and spoke in a more intimate way about educating with love and, on their own, they brought up the subject of discipline. It was completely local, and nobody said, "This is what you need to be doing." It was their own body expertise that taught them. They came up with beautiful lists of examples. Then we came back into the large group and each small group shared. They took time to listen to each other and to listen to themselves.

Afterwards, the group was energized. They said, "When can we do this again? We learned a lot today that we want to take home and practice." I told them, "I want you to go home, and every night, ask each person in your family to share one thing they were grateful for during the day. Practice that." They were excited and motivated.

Later that evening, one of the trainers hugged me in tears, saying how meaningful this process was for her. The program director told us that our approach was the only one that had really connected to the community. She said, "I have brought in many people who offered different healing approaches which didn't work for our community. The meeting you organized with local people acting as facilitators was beautiful. I could see in the faces of the men and women a certain happiness. Your approach invited their full participation and it was not complicated or threatening." The psychologist reported the parents asked, "When is the next class?"

I had never been to Mexico before; I did not speak the language. It was the language of the heart that communicated. I had only that one evening with the local people, but we were able to use *Focusing* (without the time to explain what it was) and that helped them trust their feelings. We compared and contrasted the negative experience of fear with the positive experience of love, and let the participants see that they already knew many solutions. Finally, we ended with an emphasis on the importance of gratitude.

In my workshops, I have found that emphasizing gratitude is one of the fastest ways to create a positive feeling. Gratitude is a universally understood way to concentrate on the positive points in our lives. The following activity creates a graphic visual of the balance between negative and positive yet it is simple enough to be done by children. It uses materials on hand to create a basic scale. One side of the scale symbolically holds the painful emotions and problems in their life, represented by pebbles or beans; the other side holds the blessings and positive assets, also represented by pebbles or beans. Participants are to put one pebble (or bean) on one side for each negative thing they remember. They are to put one pebble (or bean) on the other side for each positive thing they remember. Over the years, I have heard of only a few reports of the negative side being heavier than the good. For most, the exercise gives a great deal of hope and healing.

* * *

For more information:

A Primer in Positive Psychology by Christopher Peterson. (Oxford University Press, NY, 2006)

Pursuing the Good Life: 100 Reflections on Positive Psychology by Christopher Peterson. (Oxford University Press, NY, 2013)

Activity 10A: Balance of Blessings

<u>Goals:</u> To weigh the parts of our life, by balancing what we don't feel good about with what we are grateful for, and to establish hope for the future.

<u>Materials:</u> Sticks, string, circles of cloth or paper cups. Small pebbles or dried beans to place in each bag or cup.

<u>Time:</u> 45 minutes

* * *

Explain the goal of this activity. To be healthy psychologically, we need to be able to have hope for the future. We need to recognize that, even in the worst situations, there are good things in our lives. (You can refer to examples of resilience from Ch. 5.)

Divide participants into small groups of 4 to 6 people.

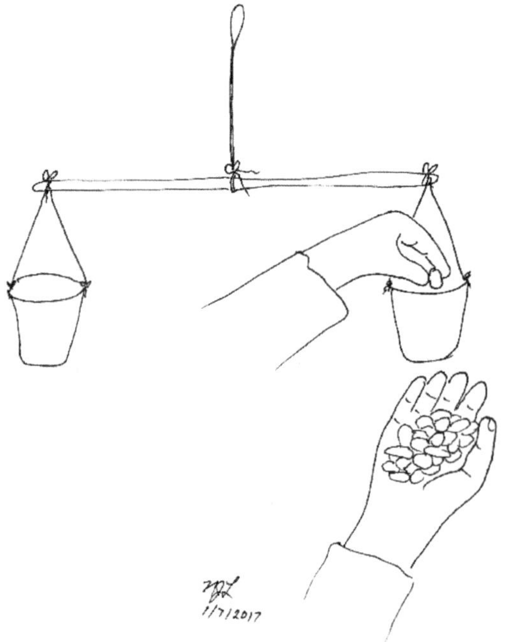

Ask each group to build a balance scale for weighing the good and the difficult in their lives.

- Each group will need a stick a little over a foot long, three pieces of string, two paper cups (or two circles of cloth plus needle and thread), and small pebbles or dried beans.

- If using cloth, make two bags by stitching around the edge of each circle and then pulling the thread. Leave an opening to insert beans or pebbles.

136

- Use two equal lengths of string to tie each bag, or each cup, to either end of the stick.
- Tie a third string in the middle of the stick and adjust it so the stick balances when hung from the middle.

When they have finished constructing the "balance scale," explain to the groups how to use it.

- Have each participant from the group take a turn while the others watch.
- On their turn, the designated participant first names negative or difficult events in their life.
- For each one, they place a pebble (or bean) in the cup. No one else in the group can help them.
- For things they are grateful for, they place a pebble (or bean) in the opposite cup. Everyone in the group is encouraged to help.

Remind them that all people, adults and children, have both good and bad reactions to the events in their lives. The scale usually tilts to the positive side; if it does not, discuss the positive points in their lives so that perhaps they can find a better balance.

When all have finished, facilitate a group discussion with the following questions:

- Which way did you expect the scale to tilt?
- Which way did it tilt?
- How might you use this scale with your community?

Note to trainer: I usually have each small group remain silent while the designated person sorts through the difficult, negative parts of her or his life, but I invite the group to join in and make suggestions for that person's positive side.

If the balance tilts towards the negative—which is unusual—you might ask probing questions in order to help the person remember something positive and add more pebbles to the "plus" side. Help them see that even in difficult circumstances, there is hope and goodness.

Activity 10B: Education/Discipline with Love

Goals: To allow parents and teachers to remember what good parenting or positive education felt like when they were young

Materials: Paper and pens (or flipcharts and markers)

Time: 45 minutes

* * *

Explain the goal of this activity. Then let the participants know that you will be doing three activities. The first will be to remember times in their childhood when they were educated through fear; the second will be to remember when they were educated using loving ways. In the third activity, they will be asked to work in small groups of 3-5 people to discuss the positive teaching methods where they felt love from their parent, guardian, or teacher.

For the first memory, invite participants to sit quietly and listen to your instructions with their eyes closed or looking down. Invite them to feel a memory of harsh discipline.

Say something like:

- I invite you to close your eyes and bring your attention into your body, first by being aware of your breathing. Take a few deep, slow breaths. (Pause to the count of 10)
- Slowly and quietly bring your attention to your feet as they rest on the floor. And sense what they feel like right now. (Pause)
- Slowly bring your awareness up your legs to your knees. Sense what your knees feel like. (Pause)

139

- Now bring your awareness to how your body rests in the chair. Notice how the chair supports your weight and how it is for you there, right now. (Pause so that the participants can feel this in their bodies)

- Now bring your awareness to your hands and arms, sensing as deeply as you can how they feel right now.

 Take time now to be aware of your shoulders and your neck. (Pause)

- Sense the back of your head, the top of your head and your face. (Pause)

- Now bring your awareness back to your breathing--don't change it, just notice it as it is. (Pause)

- Now remember a time when you were educated or disciplined through fear by your parent, relative, or teacher. Imagine how it was for you as you recall your surroundings and what was done. (Pause)

- What was that like? Maybe take a moment to remember more details of the story. (Pause for a minute)

Now take time to:

- Remember what action was taken by this person. (Pause)

- Be aware of how you know it was an action based on fear. (Pause to give people time to remember how it felt at the time)

- Notice how your body feels as you are in this memory. (Pause)

- Sense where the fear is in your body when you remember this. (Pause)

- Take a moment to really take it in and find a word or phrase or gesture that fits.

- Now open your eyes.

Invite a few participants to share what they experienced. For those who share:

- Ask if they can describe how they know it was an action based on fear.
- Invite them to share how it felt in their body.

For the second memory, repeat the instructions from the first phase of this exercise in order to guide their attention back into their bodies. Then say:

- Now I invite you to imagine how it was for you when you were educated or disciplined in a loving way by parent, teacher, or other adult. (Pause)
- Sense what that was like. Maybe take a moment to remember the story. (Pause for a minute)

Now take time to:

- Remember what action was taken by your parent, teacher, or guardian. (Pause)
- Be aware of how you know it was an action based on love. (Pause to give people time to remember how it felt at the time)
- Notice how your body feels as you are in this memory. (Pause)
- Sense where it is in your body that you feel this. (Pause)
- Take a moment to really take it in and find a word or phrase or gesture that fits.
- Now open your eyes.

Invite a few participants to share what they experienced. For those who share:

- Ask if they can describe how they know it was an action based in love.
- Invite them to share how it felt in their body.

Small Group Discussion: Divide into groups of 3-5 people. Pass out flipcharts and markers or pen and paper to each group.

Ask participants to share with their group what they learned about education with love and with fear. (15 minutes)

- Based on their shared experiences, list what parenting methods they know that are based on love and that are successful.
- What parenting methods would they like to try in their families?

After groups have made their lists, invite a spokesperson from each group to share what they came up with.

As the facilitator, end by supporting positive, resilient parenting that is based in love. You can also:

- Highlight common themes across groups.
- Invite people to add more to the lists.
- Devise something positive they can practice at home.

Note to trainer: when you lead the group into becoming aware of their body, take time to become aware of your body also. This will help you to pause an appropriate amount of time.

11. PARTICIPATORY LEARNING/THE ARTS

In participatory learning, students do not just sit passively and listen to a lecture. Rather, they contribute to the lesson in some way. These contributions are to be encouraged because people learn best by doing. To the degree that they are active, students will better remember what they have learned and will be more likely to apply it in their lives.

One of the key ways that people participate is by creating something, alone or together, which brings us to a new topic—the Arts. It is universally acknowledged that being creative relieves stress, although what constitutes "Art" varies across cultures. If your workshop is two or three days long, you will have time to include the Arts in your workshops, such as drawing, writing, drama and music. Then your participants can experience for themselves ways to release their stress and with it their emotions.

Michael Friedman says, "Art helps people to connect with and deal with their emotions. Art can help a person reach into largely unconscious parts of the mind and experience dimensions of self otherwise buried and voiceless. It can also help a person get a handle on emotions that are inarticulate. Through the arts, people can find voices to express dimensions of self usually left in silence." (*Huffington Post*, 2012)

"The idea that creative expression can make a powerful contribution to the healing process has been embraced in many different cultures." (Heather L. Stuckey and Jeremy Nobel, *The American Journal of Public Health*, 2010)

Art, drama, poetry, etc. provide opportunities for groups to bring in the wisdom of their whole being, to express what they know in colors, forms, and movements that they don't yet have words for. Our initial workshops in Pakistan were three to four days long, so we had time to experiment with various art forms. We did Drawing a Self-portrait, Mapping Resilience, Drawing Emotions, Role-playing and a movement exercise called Living Statues. (You can find a description of these in the International Rescue Committee (IRC) manual online; see references below.) Some were more successful than others. At the end of one of my three-day workshops, the participants divided into small groups and created Puppet Shows, using puppets they had made themselves. For primary school teachers, this proved to be particularly satisfying for both the teachers and their students.

Puppetry—there may be a different local term for it—is unique in that it can be used to safely address sensitive topics. It allows participants, even children, to talk about tricky issues without making them personal. Also, puppet shows combine visual and performance art in a way that is stress-free for the performer. The "actors" crouch unseen, behind a screen or table. The script is available beside them, and they can read from it as they move their puppet with a free outstretched hand. Children and grown-ups alike enjoy the performance of these shows. As such, these shows can be a valuable tool for teaching emotional skills to the wider community. One participant, after taking this workshop, had her own children make puppets whenever they were starting to get underfoot and on her nerves, in order to give their energy a better outlet.

In our workshop, the assignment was to create a show about a child who had a problem with stress, but was given a way to be resilient. The participants wrote the scripts, made their puppets with materials at hand, practiced the shows and performed them for each other. The quality of the shows was high and the messages were uplifting. The enthusiasm of the participants was noticeable.

One show featured a sad, lonely rabbit, turning to drugs which were offered him by a "hip" squirrel, who turned out *not* to be the friend he claimed to be. A pigeon helped him come back to the world of flowers and sunshine.

In another show, young Salma would not go out to the playground during recess, but preferred to sit alone in the classroom. When the teacher asked the reason, Salma explained that at home everyone called her names and said she was ugly. The teacher reflected back what Selma felt and supported Salma in finding a way she could go play with the other children and make friends.

The shows led to a lengthy discussion on the ways parents and teachers might help children deal with stress. In addition, it allowed the participants to experience what it was like to take on these various roles. By experiencing a concept they internalized it more deeply.

In this workbook, you have probably noticed several ways the activities invite participation. For instance, lecture is kept to a minimum and the workshop members are invited to participate in a variety of ways. The following participatory learning activities each have a different reason for being used.

A) I frequently suggest breaking into small groups for discussion. While some people speak easily in a large group, most prefer to contribute in a group of three to five people. I usually invite each group to write their key points on flipcharts. After the small group discussions, I ask each group to present their ideas to the entire group so that all ideas are shared. We then paste the lists on the wall, and suggest that anyone can add to it as the workshop progresses.

I will often ask the group if there is anything else, either a new idea or one that was discussed but which somehow failed to appear on a list. If there is, I add it. Writing the ideas on flipcharts is a kind of reflection—a way of showing each participant that their ideas have been heard and are acknowledged.

B) I often have the participants close their eyes and check inside, pausing to find something 'more'. *Focusing*, as I have said, cannot be learned through lecture; it *must* be experienced. Lecturing about *Focusing* is like trying to explain what something tastes like. It is far, far better to taste for yourself. That is why I frequently suggest that the group takes time to "sense inside" and to "find words and images for whatever comes," before I teach an abstract concept.

C) Brainstorming is the process of "free-listing" and is a common technique used to capture as many "out of the box" ideas as possible. In a group, one idea can lead to someone thinking of something else, so lists can become long.

Brainstorming is useful when you want to generate as many ideas as possible. I often allow participants to spontaneously call out whatever comes to mind. For the shy ones in the group, I specifically solicit their input. In some groups one person can tend to overwhelm others, so I might go around the room (one person at a time) asking for ideas. No matter which method I use, *all* ideas are collected and recorded. No idea is too crazy. None are turned down or critiqued; every input is welcomed.

By deferring judgment and reaching for quantity, you stimulate creative thinking. Later, the ideas can be sorted out for actual use. It is also useful, when sorting, to take a moment with what seems at first glance to be a "silly" idea. If you ask for the "more" behind the idea, you will often find a fresh approach to the situation being brainstormed.

D) Of course, I include the Arts. The activity can be as simple as having everyone draw their *Calm Place*. It can be as complicated as doing a puppet show. Artistic expression finds unique expression in each culture, and each community varies. You, the trainer, need to find a culturally comfortable way to include Arts in your activities.

As you adapt these modules to the needs of your community, be sure to include participatory learning activities (PLA's). Each method has value, but the important thing is to vary them because participants will tire of one style if it is repeated too often. IRC has developed a list of these activities (given in Handout 11A), and you may want to teach this principle to your class, especially if they are going to facilitate future classes.

Of the items listed on Handout 11A, role playing, skits, and puppet shows are the most powerful. They allow the "actors" to empathize with their characters, or to experience for a moment what their characters might feel. Dramatic presentations are especially useful for review. They can pull together the essence of what has been taught. Although a good project can take all afternoon, it can help participants consider many aspects of what they have learned and then, as a bonus, they can share what they have created by performing for others.

Role play takes the least amount of time and has already been described in Activity 9C. In this chapter, two additional drama activities are described, Activity 11A and 11B, and a bonus self-portrait Activity 11C..

* * *

For more information:

An excellent, longer list of participatory learning techniques can be found through a Micro Finance Corporation site under their Participatory Action Research:
> http://www.gdrc.org/icm/ppp/plt.html

The International Rescue Committee manual has the following additional art-based activities: Mapping Resilience (p.26), Living Statues (p.36), Drawing Emotions (p. 63); Role-play Emotions (p. 64). The IRC manual can be found at:
> http://healingclassrooms.org/downloads/Addressing_Afg_Childrens_
> Psychosocial_Needs.pdf

Activity 11A: Skits

<u>Goals:</u> To learn about giving someone Emotional First Aid through using listening skills

<u>Time:</u> 2+ hours

Instructions:

- Have the participants divide into small groups of three people each. Have them come up with a story about listening and communicating, and write down words to say. The story must include someone who is emotionally upset. What does the other person say to 'help?' What do they say that does not help? (30 min)
- Give them time to practice. (30 min)
- Let everyone perform for the entire group. (40+ min)
- Allow time for discussion of the issues raised. (20 min)

Note to trainer: Note that Skits take about half the time of Puppet Shows, but twice the amount of time as Role Plays.

Activity 11B: Puppet Shows

<u>Goal</u>: To teach about Stress and Resilience

<u>Time</u>: 3+ hours

<u>Materials</u>: cloth, sticks, rags, yarn, tape, stapler, colored pens, old baby clothes, paper

Instructions:

- Have the participants divide into small groups of three people each and come up with a story around a topic such as stress being changed to resilience, as described in the chapter above (30 min). Have them write down words to say.

- Make the puppets, perhaps as an overnight assignment. The only rule is that the puppets be hand-made from available materials; no one is to buy anything.

- Give them time to practice. (30 min)

- Let everyone perform for the entire group. (40 min+)

- Allow time for discussion of the issues raised. (20 min)

Activity 11C: Self-Portrait

<u>Goal</u>: Explore positive self-awareness

<u>Time</u>: 30 minutes

<u>Materials</u>: Colored pencils, crayons, drawing paper

Instructions:

Explain the goal of this activity. One goal can be to facilitate general
introductions of participants.

- Distribute paper and colored pencils or crayons.
- Ask participants to draw or color a picture of themselves. Ask them to
write at least 3 things they like about themselves on the picture, focusing on
positive aspects--skills, looks, personality, or intelligence.
- Ask them to share their pictures.
- Facilitate a group discussion about what has been learned from the
activity:
    - Describe what is in your picture. What is positive?
    - Is it easy to describe positive aspects about yourself? Why or why
    not?
    - How might you share this activity?

Note to trainer:

Keep in mind that participants might find it difficult to identify positive aspects
of themselves. They are not to identify what they can *do* but what they *are,*
including characteristics of themselves that they like. Give them time. One way
to help them is first to have them identify positive aspects of each other.

Handout 11A: Participatory Learning Activities

Brainstorming—generally done in large group. All participants are given a chance to contribute ideas concerning a problem or topic. The contributions are recorded on flipcharts at the front of the room. The aim is to get quantity, not quality. In order to encourage creative flow, each person's view is accepted without judgment. By getting as many ideas as possible, new and unrealized possibilities can be discovered.

"Yes, and..." This is done during a discussion or brainstorming session. Each person's views are accepted ("Yes") and something more is needed, ("and..."). This encouragement provides that the discussion (or the brainstorming) is both positive *and* constructive.

Visualizations: Allow participants some quiet time to image what something would be like for them. This inner work is very productive for sensing into emotions and attitudes such as respect or contentment. It is also good for imagining an ideal and getting a bodily feeling of success; for imagining what that participant wants to achieve, and getting a bodily feeling of a plan.

Small group work gives each participant a chance to contribute his or her ideas. In addition, complex ideas can be broken down and groups can be given different parts of the same problem (or different aspects of the same issue).

Assignments can be given to small groups to discuss on their own.

Daily activity profile. This is a calendar of activities that a person does in the day/week/month/year. One purpose might be gender awareness—who gets up first, each activity, who goes to bed last. Draw pictures or write; men can write this too. Another purpose might be times of day when Focusing might be useful. Map out the day and when awareness might be good, such as when the kids are coming home from school and are tired.

Time line. Ask the members to draw a line and mark on it the major events in the community with the approximate dates. Discuss the changes that have occurred.

Art, drama, poetry etc. These provide opportunities for groups to bring in the wisdom of their whole being, to express what they know in colors, forms, and movements that they don't yet have words for. The arts work especially well to summarize ideas and concepts at the end of the day or the end of the workshop. The more aspects in which a problem is considered, the more the participants will retain what they have learned.

> **Some examples:**
> - Draw a picture of your inside place with guests
> - Make group picture of the stress in your community
> - Write a song or poem about how you feel now, compared with how you felt at the beginning of the workshop
> - Draw a picture of your emotions—use colors
> - Perform puppet shows about stress, showing good and bad kinds
> - Put on skits about gratitude and ingratitude
> - Role play "listening" and "not listening"

12. EVALUATION

In 2013, I traveled to Tokyo to work with Japanese professor Mako Hikasa and her students. Together, we were able to offer workshops to survivors of the great tsunami of 2011 and the ensuing Fukushima disaster when people fled the radioactive effects of the nuclear power plant explosion. In a variety of presentation formats, from lectures on *Community Wellness Focusing* to both Focusers and professionals, to local meetings with disaster survivors, we reached more than 350 individuals, including university faculty, graduate students, psychologists, community leaders, and many survivors.

On evaluation forms, attendees expressed a more than 97% rate of satisfaction with the workshops and said that they found the concepts useful in their daily life. The long-term impact of these programs was evaluated at a round-table discussion at the 33rd Conference of the Japanese Association for Humanistic Psychology in September 2014 (3.24-3.90, on a 1-4 scale). The discussion revealed that *Community Wellness Focusing* had inspired many subsequent new developments in ways to teach Focusing and help traumatized citizens. [Mako Hikasa and Kazuyoshi Nakamura. "The Effect of introducing *Community Wellness Focusing* into Japan," The Japanese Association for Humanistic Psychology 33th Conference Program and Presentation Proceedings, Nanzan University, October 11-13, 2014, pp. 62-63.]

In Afghanistan, the success of *Community Wellness Focusing* programs was evaluated by independent researchers for three groups: Physiotherapy and

Rehabilitation Services for Afghanistan, The Noor Education Center, and the International Rescue Committee. The following outcomes were identified:

- Reduced violence in families and schools
- Improvements in wellbeing and physical health
- Reduced reliance on alcohol or drugs, both illegal and over-the-counter
- Increased capacity to facilitate peace and reconciliation

One remarkable aspect of CWF projects is the way they naturally expand as more and more individuals in a country or region attend workshops and return to their communities to put their new skills into practice.

The number of people served directly by workshops in Afghanistan between 2004 and 2009 were 3,047 individuals. But that is not the whole story. Many trainees returned to their villages and introduced *Focusing*, resiliency, and stress management into their schools and communities, and from there into individual homes, significantly impacting the daily lives of additional thousands.

For an estimate of numbers benefitting indirectly, we might multiply 3,047 (my original trainees) by 6 (the average size of an Afghan family), which equals 18,282 people. As it happened, 2,029 of those trained at that time were teachers. We can assume that each teacher works with about 40 students per year. We know that many of those students took home what they learned and shared it with their parents and siblings. If just one fourth of the students shared the teachings, that would be 2,029 (teachers) x 10 (one fourth of their students) x 6 (average family size) or an additional 122,000 people. This may seem like an exaggeration, but another 10,000 teachers were reached in an earlier training for UNICEF IN 2002. And training in CWF and psychosocial wellness has continued.

In order to evaluate the success of each project, I encourage each local project leader to set specific goals for their group, based on an assessment of local needs. I encourage them to ask community members what they hope to achieve and how they will know when it is accomplished. Pre- and post-tests are then designed to provide self-assessments of relevant skills, attitudes, and practices. Where possible, these outcomes can be measured at six-month intervals over a period of several years to determine the endurance of change. We have found it useful for trainers of different CWF programs to use a common form to evaluate their projects (see Handout 12A).

In Afghanistan, one trainer created an evaluation form for participants that gave helpful results (Handout 12B). Her four-day training was called "The Psychosocial and *Focusing* Workshop" and was held in the spring of 2002 for 21 Afghan teachers at IRC's girls' school for Afghan refugees living in Pakistan— part of their female education program. The 21 answers to the evaluation questions are combined into the following answers (translated from Dari):

Question 1: Did you find the workshop effective/useful?

All answers were "Yes".

Follow up to question 1: Why?

Participants' answers: (merged)

> Because it offered a lot of valuable new information and had
> many interesting activities. Every topic was relevant to our
> daily lives. This workshop will no doubt help us bring
> considerable changes in our own as well as the children's lives.

By attending this workshop, we realized that we have not had appropriate behavior with our own children. If the teachers incorporate all these topics and activities in their lessons, they will certainly be able to help the traumatized children.

Question 2: Which topics of the workshop did you like the most and which ones were not interesting?

Participants' answers: (merged)

All topics were interesting and informative particularly the scale of blessings, puppet shows, relaxation and Focusing techniques, stress, resiliency and what is normal for Afghan society. There was no topic in the workshop that was not interesting and that we disliked.

Question 3: Which topics were difficult and therefore you will need more training?

Participants' answers: (merged)

Majority answered that all topics were easy and well understood. The trainers facilitated the sessions with exceptional skill and expertise, which resulted in an excellent delivery of information from the trainers to the participants. Some of the participants said that at the beginning, the workshop seemed difficult, but later it got easier. Others commented that when a session started, they thought that it would be very difficult and they would not be able to participate or do what the trainer was asking. They were surprised to see that they really did what they thought they wouldn't be able to do.

The activities on resiliency and what is normal were very difficult at the beginning, but as the activities were explained repeatedly and shown on the lines and charts, they became clear.

A number of participants wrote that some topics were difficult and they would need more training. These were the exercises on resiliency, stress (and how to manage it), Afghan society norms of behavior, how to determine the deviations a child might have in various ways from his/her society's norms and how to help him/her.

Question 4: Will the workshop have any effects on your own life? Can you give examples?

Participants' answers: (merged)

The workshop will have considerable positive effects on our lives. For example, it changed our way of thinking as we learned that one should not always focus on negative aspects of life, but should also remember the positive ones. Now we know how to cope with stress and relax when we are tense and under pressure. In addition, it will help us change our inappropriate behavior and attitudes toward our children.

Question 5: What suggestions would you make to further improve the training?

Participants' answers (merged)

> Some participants suggested that the timing of the workshop
> should be reconsidered. It is good to finish the training daily at
> 2:00pm, which will give them some time to do their other office
> work. In addition, attending a full day training is tiring,
> especially after lunch when it is difficult to be attentive and
> active in the class. Other participants said that the days of the
> workshop should be increased.

> One suggestion said that work can be split between groups. For
> example, in one exercise, all four groups listed (a) —activities
> that teachers can use . . . to improve their own psychosocial
> well-being and then (b) —activities that teachers can use to
> help children improve their psychosocial well-being. It would
> be better if two groups worked on (a) and two groups worked
> on (b). This would help avoid repetition and save time.

Question 6: In your opinion, which topics are more important for teachers and
students and can help them?

Participants' answers (merged)

> All topics are important and helpful for teachers and children
> especially the norms of Afghan society, resiliency, puppet show,
> stress symptoms and stress management, relaxation and

focusing techniques. All these will help teachers improve their own psychosocial well-being, as well as better respond to the psychosocial needs of the children.

HANDOUT 12A: Trainer Evaluation Form

Class	Trainer	Date	Topics	Observations: include changes in behaviors, key learning, interesting stories and quotes.					

HANDOUT 12B: Participant Evaluation Form

1. Was the workshop effective/useful?

2. Which topics of the workshop were the most interesting/useful?

3. Which topics of the workshop were the least interesting/useful?

4. Which topics were difficult and therefore you will need more training?

5. Will the workshop have any effect on your own life? Can you give examples?

6. What suggestions would you make to improve the training?

7. Which topics are more important for the communities/people with whom you work?

Focusing Initiatives International

Recognizing the growth of interest in community resilience and *Community Wellness Focusing*, Pat Omidian and Melinda Darer in 2014 decided to establish a non-profit organization to further this work.

They knew they had formed an ideal partnership.

Melinda had just resigned from her 17-year position as Managing Director at The International Focusing Institute, where she had worked closely with the founders, Dr. Eugene Gendlin and his wife, Dr. Mary Hendricks Gendlin. During her tenure there, Melinda had developed both strategies and programs. She had increased staff (4x), multiplied the revenue (8x), and expanded the membership (8x). She had also networked extensively with Focusers worldwide and collaborated with international organizations in Argentina, Australia, Canada, China, Ecuador, Germany, Israel, Italy, Palestine, the Netherlands, and the United States.

Pat had almost thirty years of direct, hands-on experience working with communities from the Middle East, Afghanistan, Pakistan, and Japan. People trained by Pat have reached out to train others in a widening circle of Community Wellness practice. To date, thousands of teachers and social workers in these countries have received instruction in listening, basic *Focusing* and psychosocial support.

Together with Nina Joy Lawrence, Pat played a major role in the development of the theory and practice of *Community Wellness Focusing*. Their work was heavily influenced by such pioneers in the field as Anna Willman, who now serves on the FII Board.

Since its inception, Focusing Initiatives International's mission has been to provide a resource for communities suffering from the stresses of war, natural disasters, endemic poverty, epidemics, and all forms of violence or social injustice. FII recognizes that it is essential to adapt and infuse the life-forward practice of Focusing in order to have it accepted into the local culture.

We work to ensure cultural relevance and to support local leadership through a process of deep listening and learning from members of the community. Then we develop trainings, mentoring, and follow-up measures based on local needs and conditions.

The Focusing Initiatives team bases its work on the following discoveries:

- An individual's health is directly connected to and impacted by the health of the community

- Solutions to local problems already exist locally

- People can be creative when their culture is honored

- When *Focusing* is introduced in a culturally appropriate context, it not only helps traumatized people find their way forward, but also promotes resiliency in the community as a whole

Focusing Initiatives International seeks to identify communities that can benefit from this process. In some cases, a community asks us for support; in others cases we initiate the process. Our sliding scale fees enable us to reach those communities where the need is greatest.

Through its organizational umbrella, team members provide mentoring to community workers throughout the world. We teach *Focusing*, stress management, and other principles included in this workbook, which aid in self-reflection, communication, and better listening. Trained staff offer technical assistance to design, fund, and operate local programs. The population served by FII includes:

- Members of communities in distress throughout the world

- Those who are working in the many projects that already exist in these communities and who wish to strengthen their work by incorporating our program

- Those who wish to initiate new projects using this process

All projects are collaborative. In the first three years of its existence, FII established connections with and provided support to people doing creative and healing work in Afghanistan, Australia, Belgium, Canada, China, Finland, France, Germany, Italy, Japan, Liberia, Mexico, Nepal, The Netherlands, New Zealand, Pakistan, Spain, Switzerland, Tunisia, UK and the US.

FII's goal is for each project to become self-supporting both in leadership and finances. FII will do everything it can to help each one to achieve that status. Please visit our website and/or contact us for more information.

www.focusinginternational.org

Melinda Darer: Melinda@focusinginternational.org

Pat Omidian: Pat@focusinginternational.org